D0621037

This book is a gift from the
Range Conservation Foundation
made possible by funding from the
Laura Moore Cunningham
Foundation

Reflections of the West

Cowboy painters and poets

Eight Saddles Bein' Sat
By Don Weller

Published by Range Conservation Foundation & RANGE magazine
C.J. Hadley, publisher/editor

"I loved that ranch, though sometimes it did seem that instead of us owning the place, the place owned us."

JEANNETTE WALLS
"HALF BROKE HORSES"

Cowboy
By Jim Rey

PUBLISHER/EDITOR: C.J. Hadley
ART DIRECTOR: John Bardwell
FIELD EDITOR: Carolyn Dufurrena
EDITORIAL ASSISTANT: Ann Galli
PROOFREADER: Denyse Pellettieri White

Publication of this book was made possible by generous donations from people who care about the American West, with special assistance from Margo Metegrano of CowboyPoetry.com, Jerry Brooks, Joel Nelson, Vess Quinlan and Randy Rieman.

Library of Congress Cataloging-in-Publication Data
Hadley, C.J.
Reflections of the West: Cowboy painters and poets
Caroline Joy Hadley
ISBN 978-D-9647456-6-7
LCCN 2015945674

Published by Range Conservation Foundation & RANGE magazine, Carson City, Nevada.

$43 U.S.A.
Printed in China
Copyright © 2015 Range Conservation Foundation & RANGE magazine

Site and Sound

By C.J. Hadley

Buffalo Bill bronc rider, Harry Webb, said "Cowboy life is good, bad and plain hell." This book shares all three.

"Reflections of the West" is the sequel to "Brushstrokes & Balladeers: Painters and poets of the American West," which was called "stunningly beautiful" and "an eclectic masterpiece."

In 2014, "Brushstrokes" won the prestigious Wrangler award from the National Cowboy & Western Heritage Museum in Oklahoma City and the Will Rogers Gold Medallion in Fort Worth for "Best Poetry Book of the Year."

This tome, "Reflections of the West: Cowboy painters and poets," includes work from fifty-three poets and thirty painters. Many are multiple award winners. Writers with Pulitzers, several state Poet Laureates, and painters with too many honors to mention. Accolades from around the world.

The creators in this book, either born to the ranching life or with gifts extraordinary enough to be able to share it, all have something in common.

Cowboys and cowgirls.

You will find that there is nothing fake about real cowboy life. It isn't a way to get rich. And, often thanks to Mother Nature, it isn't easy. But very few who have lived and worked horseback would ever want to change it.

Curley Fletcher said: "I spent the best years as a cowboy of the old school. I still look back to long days and nights in the saddle, at thirty dollars a month, as the happiest of my existence."

Look and listen…and by the end of this book, you will catch a glimpse of the reason why.

> ## "Do not let any sweet-talking woman beguile your good sense with the fascinations of her shape. It's your barn she's after."
>
> HESIOD, "WORKS AND DAYS"
> 8TH CENTURY B.C.

Aloft on the Dancy
By Nancy Boren

3

Canyon Country
By Jason Rich

POETS

Grave Error
By S. Omar Barker

Boot Hill was the payoff,
them old-timers claim,
for men that pulled triggers
without takin' aim!

Suffolk Sheep
By Jan Perkins

(Continued)

> "A farm of your own is better, even if small,
> everyone's someone at home;
> though he has two goats and a coarsely roofed house,
> that is better than begging."

12TH CENTURY ICELANDIC
"SAYINGS OF THE HIGH ONE (HÁVAMÁL)"

Tight Dally
By C.M. Russell
(1864–1926)

PAINTERS

Rhymes of the Ranges

By Bruce Kiskaddon
(1878-1950)

These are just a few rhymes of old friends and old times,
    And I hope before I am through—
Just once in a while they will bring a broad smile,
    To the face of some old buckaroo.

Wherever he worked in the days that are past,
    On the mountain, the plain or the valley,
What matters is now if he tied hard and fast,
    Or tumbled his steer with a dally.

If he wrangled the bunch, if he rode gentle strings,
    If he topped off the wild ones that shimmy—
If he rode with his leathers through centre fire rings,
    Or sat on a double-rigged rimmy.

If he worked for big outfits far out on the plains,
    Where they never had use for a packer,
Or back in the hills in the snow and the rains,
    With the regular old greasy sacker.

If he worked as a drifter and trusted to luck,
    If he managed a bunch of his own,
If he cooked at the wagon and put up the chuck,
    Or held down a line camp alone.

They are plain simple tales, of the round-ups and trails,
    When he worked on the range with the cattle:
Not of wild woolly nights, nor of gambling hall fights,
    But the days and the nights in the saddle.

This poem is entitled "Introductory" and is from Bruce Kiskaddon's
"Rhymes of the Ranges," published in 1924.

Throwing a Fit
By J.N. Swanson
(1927-2014)

Ridin' With Ol' Figment

By Joel Nelson

I rode beside him several years
Or was it just one day
Out here I've found that calendars
And clocks get in the way

Time was of no consequence
We rode 'til we got through
"Just listen to the cattle, boy
They'll tell you what to do."

"Just listen to the cattle, boy—
They'll tell you where to be
Pay attention to the cow up front
Instead of watching me."

"Listen to that brindle, boy—
She's cunning and deceiving
You'd best be making plans because
She's telling you she's leaving."

"Some fellers call 'em stupid—
Boy, don't even get me started—
That's what they'll likely say
Just after they have been outsmarted."

"Don't be asking me now, boy
I'm just a dumb old cuss—
Let the cattle tell you how
They got more sense than us."

"I ain't drawin' pay to school on you
So don't be askin' me—
I'm just a daywork cowboy
Ask the high-horned Ph.D."

To all the million questions posed
Regarding why and how
The answer was predictable
"Boy, listen to the cow!"

I rode beside him all one day
Or was it all year long
It's sorta coming back to me
But wait I could be wrong

The best way to explain it
He's a voice inside my head
He'd show up when I worked alone
I'd hang on what he said

My imaginary mentor
No one else could hear or see
Who taught me most of what I know
As he trailed along with me

He rode beside me all those years
He's here beside me now
And thanks to him I learned a lot
Just listening to a cow

Heading Up French Glen
By William Matthews

The Story of Mongrel Grey

By Banjo Paterson (1864-1941)

This is the story the stockman told,
    On the cattle camp, when the stars were bright;
The moon rose up like a globe of gold
    And flooded the plain with her mellow light.
We watched the cattle till dawn of day
And he told me the story of Mongrel Grey.

"He was a knock-about station hack,
    Spurned and walloped, and banged and beat;
Ridden all day with a sore on his back,
    Left all night with nothing to eat.
That was a matter of everyday—
Common occurrence to Mongrel Grey.

"Pr'aps we'd have sold him, but someone heard
    He was bred out back on a flooded run,
Where he learnt to swim like a water bird,
    Midnight or midday were all as one.
In the flooded ground he could find his way,
Nothing could puzzle old Mongrel Grey.

"'Tis a special gift that some horses learn,
    When the floods are out they will splash along
In girth-deep water, and twist and turn
    From hidden channel and billabong.
Never mistaking the road to go,
For a man may guess—but the horses *know*.

"I was camping out with my youngest son
    —Bit of a nipper just learnt to speak—
In an empty hut on the lower run,
    Shooting and fishing in Conroy's Creek.
The youngster toddled about all day,
And with our horses was Mongrel Grey.

"All of a sudden the flood came down
    Fresh from the hills with the mountain rain,
Roaring and eddying, rank and brown,
    Over the flats and across the plain.
Rising and falling—fall of night—
Nothing but water appeared in sight.

"'Tis a nasty place when the floods are out,
    Even in daylight, for all around
Channels and billabongs twist about,

Stretching for miles in the flooded ground.
And to move was a hopeless thing to try
In the dark, with the water just racing by.

"I had to try it. I heard a roar,
    And the wind swept down with the blinding rain;
And the water rose till it reached the floor
    Of our highest room, and 'twas very plain
The way the water was sweeping down
We must shift for the highlands at once, or drown.

"Off to the stable I splashed, and found
    The horses shaking with cold and fright;
I led them down to the lower ground,
    But never a yard would they swim that night!
They reared and snorted and turned away,
And none would face it but Mongrel Grey.

"I bound the child on the horse's back,
    And we started off with a prayer to Heaven,
Through the rain and the wind and the pitchy black,
    For I knew that the instinct God has given
To guide His creatures by night and day
Would lead the footsteps of Mongrel Grey.

"He struck deep water at once and swam—
    I swam beside him and held his mane—
Till we touched the bank of the broken dam
    In shallow water—then off again,
Swimming in darkness across the flood,
Rank with the smell of the drifting mud.

"He turned and twisted across and back,
    Choosing the places to wade or swim.
Picking the safest and shortest track,
    The pitchy darkness was clear to him.
Did he strike the crossing by sight or smell?
The Lord that led him alone could tell!

"He dodged the timber whene'er he could,
    But the timber brought us to grief at last;
I was partly stunned by a log of wood,
    That struck my head as it drifted past;
And I lost my grip of the brave old grey,
And in half a second he swept away.

Racing the Wind
By Karen G. Myers

"I reached a tree, where I had to stay,
    And did'n' perish for two days hard;
And lived on water—but Mongrel Grey,
    He walked right into the homestead yard
At dawn next morning, and grazed around,
With the child on top of him safe and sound.

"We keep him now for the wife to ride,
    Nothing too good for him now of course;
Never a whip on his fat old hide,
    For she owes the child to that old grey horse.
And not Old Tyson himself could pay
The purchase money of Mongrel Grey."

Eminent Domain

By Wally McRae

Wally McRae
By William Matthews

From the Highland Sod, with faith in God,
To this land, young and profane,
Grandad was drawn, long ere the dawn
Of Eminent Domain.

With no regrets he paid his debts,
Fought the elements to remain.
Each challenge met, long before the threat
Of Eminent Domain.

This land's been wet by my father's sweat,
His bones lie 'neath this plain.
But you'd rip in, with your dust and din,
And Eminent Domain.

My mother's tears and unspoken fears
That she always fought to restrain.
Did she somehow hear, and come to fear
Your Eminent Domain?

"Public need" we're advised to heed,
But it somehow comes out, "private gain."
You play the rune. Do we dance to the tune
Of Eminent Domain?

You praise to the skies, "Free Enterprise,"
Curse the government as your bane.
But you're quick to use, or even abuse,
Her Eminent Domain.

You pandering blights! Don't tell me of your rights.
Rights and obligations are twain.
Land's earned by sweat and love—not threat
Of Eminent Domain!

I'll not cower from lines of pipe and power
Or twin scythes of rail for your train.
Understand me full well. You can go to hell
With your Eminent Domain.

The Outlaw

By Badger Clark (1883-1957)

When my loop takes hold on a two year old
By the feet or the neck or the horn,
He can plunge and fight till his eyes go white
But I'll throw him as sure as you're born.
Tho the taut rope sings like a banjo string
And the latigoes creak and strain,
Yet I've got no fear of an outlaw steer
And I'll tumble him on the plain.

For a man is a man and a steer is a beast
And the man is boss of the herd
And each of the bunch, from the biggest to least
Must come down when he says the word.

When my leg swings 'cross on an outlaw hawse
And my spurs clinch into his hide,
He can r'ar and pitch over hill and ditch,
But wherever he goes, I'll ride.
Let 'im spin and flop like a crazy top
Or flit like a wind-whipped smoke,
But he'll know the feel of my rowelled heel
Till he's happy to own he's broke

For a man is a man and a hawse is a brute,
And the hawse may be prince of his clan,
But he'll bow to the bit and the steel-shod boot
And own that his boss is the man.

When the devil at rest underneath my vest
Gets up and begins to paw,
And my hot tongue strains at its bridle-reins,
Then I tackle the real outlaw;
When I get plumb riled and my sense goes wild,
And my temper has fractious growed,
If he'll hump his neck just a triflin' speck,
Then it's dollars to dimes I'm throwed.

For a man is a man, but he's partly a beast—
He can brag till he makes you deaf,
But the one lone brute, from the west to the east,
That he can't quite break is himse'f.

A Moment of Great Peril in a Cowboy's Career
By C.M. Russell
(1864-1926)

This painting was used on the cover of Leslie's Weekly,
March 24, 1904. Price 10 cents.

The Shank of the Evening

By Red Steagall

That new batch of heifers we got in today
Come off of the truck in a run.
They scattered and split like a covey of quail
We're lucky, we found every one.

Got talked into them by a trader last week.
I wonder if I'm still the boss.
South Georgia can keep all them rats with long ears.
I like Hereford and Black Angus cross.

Fading Light
By Tom Browning

The grass in the meadow is starting to burn,
Gets brown just a little each day.
If we'd get a rain by the end of the month,
I'd still get a cutting of hay.

We got a good shower the middle of March,
Was dry as a bone up till then.
It's the third week of June, we ain't had one since.
It may never rain here again.

I guess if I'se up to my stirrups in mud
I'd think there's a drought on the way.
If it rains for a week, it still ain't enough.
I'm lookin' for clouds every day.

I'm grateful as hell for the moisture I get.
I reckon I get my fair share,
But I like my mama cows rollin' in fat.
Without rain they're nothin' but hair.

The breeze 'cross the back porch is coolin' things down.
My yeller dog's lickin' my hand.
He knows when I worry 'bout cattle and rain,
No one but him understands.

The coyotes are startin' to yip at the moon.
The yeller dog joins in the fun.
He's brave as a bear when they're out on the hill,
They challenge him, he'll turn and run.

Hey, life ain't so tough, we got our own place.
The missus ain't cranky with me.
The kids are all growed up and gone off to school.
We're happy as we want to be.

Yes, this time of day is real special to me.
It's when I reshuffle my load.
I add it all up, and come out way ahead
When daylight's been saucered and blowed.

In the shank of the evenin' I boil it all down
To the basics, there ain't nothin' more.
We've got a good life and we like it out here.
The tough times just even the score.

We could sell this old homestead and move into town
But what in the hell would I do,
In the shank of the evenin', fight traffic and noise?
No thank you, I'll tough this one through.

High O' Silver
By Steven Saylor

Just Think

By Robert W. Service (1874-1958)

Just think! some night the stars will gleam
    Upon a cold, grey stone,
And trace a name with silver beam,
    And lo! 'twill be your own.

That night is speeding on to greet
    Your epitaphic rhyme.
Your life is but a little beat
    Within the heart of Time.

A little gain, a little pain,
    A laugh, lest you may moan;
A little blame, a little fame,
    A star-gleam on a stone.

Where the Ponies Come to Drink

By Henry Herbert Knibbs (1874-1945)

Up in Northern Arizona there's a Ranger trail that passes
Through a mesa, like a faery lake with pines upon its brink,
And across the trail a stream runs all but hidden in the grasses,
Till it finds an emerald hollow where the ponies come to drink.

Out they fling across the mesa, windblown manes and forelocks dancing,
—Blacks and sorrels, bays and pintos, wild as eagles, eyes agleam;
From their hoofs the silver flashes, burning beads and arrows glancing
Through the bunchgrass and the gramma, as they cross the little stream.

Down they swing as if pretending, in their orderly disorder,
That they stopped to hold a powwow, just to rally for the charge
That will take them, close to sunset, twenty miles across the border;
Then the leader sniffs and drinks with forefeet planted on the marge.

One by one each head is lowered, till some yearling nips another,
And the playful interruption starts an eddy in the band:
Snorting, squealing, plunging, wheeling, round they circle in a smother
Of the muddy spray, nor pause until they find the firmer land.

My old cow horse, he runs with 'em: turned him loose for good last season;
Eighteen years' hard work, his record, and he's earned his little rest;
And he's taking it by playing, acting proud, and with good reason;
Though he's starched a little forward, he can fan it with the best.

Once I called him—almost caught him, when he heard my spur-chains jingle;
Then he eyed me some reproachful, as if making up his mind:
Seemed to say, "Well, if I have to—but you know I'm living single…"
So I laughed. In just a minute he was pretty hard to find.

Some folks wouldn't understand it—writing lines about a pony—
For a cow horse is a cow horse—nothing else, most people think—
But for eighteen years your pardner, wise and faithful, such a crony
Seems worth watching for a spell, down where the ponies come to drink.

Cool Clear Water (Woodcut)
By Steven Saylor

From "Songs of the Outlands," 1914

Once in a Blue Moon

By Joel Nelson

Do you think that it might be all over
Have you ever felt we've moved beyond
Where just merely being "out there"
Touched by some strange magic wand

Leaving us hypnotized by the riding
For some baron with a brand
No longer fills all our senses
And no longer feels quite as grand?

Have we lost that youthful innocence
Like the young horses that we've tamed
With no nonsense left in either
Are our days no longer framed

By the morning star and sunset
Holding herd in cold, dust, and damp
Out beyond the reach of the highlines
In some wild high lonesome camp?

God! It's not that we aren't still able
We've ascended up to the rank
Of the lofty and the exalted
But we poured our wine and we drank

Through the roundups and the seasons
'Til the wonder of it all ceased
Now our goblets stand half empty
And the muses have released

All our tired and weary tribesmen
Of that aged horseback mob
From the lust for pure horseback living
And the true straight riding job

Now we're more for the smooth and the quiet
And we're less for the reckless and wild
Looking more through the eyes of the steady
And less through the eyes of the child—

Shaking heads at the young and flamboyant,
At the loud, at the brash, at the bold—
Disregarding we once might have been there
Not acknowledging that we've grown old.

And yet once in a blue moon we'll weaken
And the clan blood will surge in our veins
And we'll hire on to brand with the wagon
And our hands will feel young on the reins

And our youth will return with the season
Like the sap rising strong in the grass
Yes our youth will come back with the greenup
Just like sap rising strong in the grass!

**Remember
Back When?**
By S.C. Mummert

Friendly Persuasion
By Jim Rey

Plum Blossoms in the Spring

By Yvonne Hollenbeck

When at first I married this cowboy I had a lot to learn
about the style of life he lives and the money that we'd earn.
We married in the summer and it soon was in the fall
when I thought that I knew everything, was sure I knew it all.

After all I'd drove a tractor and learned to mow and rake
I only wiped two gate posts out but he did not hesitate
to have me checking pastures, even helped him pull a well;
of course we had some arguments, but that part I won't tell.

It soon got close to Christmas, our first one since we'd wed,
and I had hopes for real nice gifts, but I got a card instead.
That winter was a bad one, we got a lot of snow
and seemed like every morning it was at least fifteen below.

I learned to start cold tractors, not a very easy task,
and chop holes in a frozen tank with a dull and heavy ax;
I figured after all this work I'd done through thick and thin,
that I'd get a real nice Valentine, but I was wrong again.

What got me most, a friend of mine got flowers and a ring
(her husband's secret lady-friend received the same darned thing)
and I realized how lucky I was to have the man I got,
'cause we all know in everything the cream comes to the top.

He told me how he hates to shop, and usually short on cash
but to buy whatever I might need and I don't need to ask.
Then I was taken back a bit when he did the nicest thing;
we were really busy calving on a real nice day that spring.

It was getting late that afternoon, when I saw him riding in;
he rode down to the garden where I was and then he grinned.
A big bouquet of plum blossoms he handed me, then said:
"I've never bought you flowers, but I cut you some instead."

Many years have come and gone and I know I've been blessed
to be married to this cowboy 'cause to me he is the best;
though he don't spend money buying gifts and costly things,
he makes me feel real special with plum blossoms every spring.

The Honeymoon
By Bonnie Conrad

Cloud Waves

By John Dofflemyer

Forecasts vary, computer models change:
dry rain of fiery leaves, stirred and torn
from the honey locust tree, cloud waves

in all shades of gray—a dark flotilla
peeks over the ridge for ships run aground
against the Sierra's leaking cargo low

on Blue Ridge trimmed with a white ribbon.
We sip whiskey, replay the week and squeal
like children on each gust, tip our glasses

to the work got done. To herds of virgins
readied for the Wagyu bulls, gentle ladies
churning under a full moon. To the mothers

with first calves driven up canyon, now
grazing the north slopes as it tries to rain.
To the four we couldn't find by day:

awakened by their bawling for babies,
night lit by the moon, they awaited
dawn at the gate while we slept easily.

Maybe It Will Be A Good Year
By Tim Cox

**Occasionally
I Ran Into
An Old Vaquero**
By J.N. Swanson
(1927-2014)

John Cutler's Cowboys

By John Dofflemyer

*"We at last struck a trail that has recently been cut for the
purpose of bringing in cattle. It is at an altitude of 7,800
feet. Here is a succession of grassy meadows—one called
Big Meadow is several miles in extent."*
        —William H. Brewer, 18 June 1864

I know the place
my grandfather's grandfather found
to escape the drought, heard the voices

of his vaqueros when I got turned around
in the tight pines near Ellis Meadow—easy
to lose yourself and time altogether—feel

them close to the black rings of stone.
Up from Eshom where the Yokuts held
their last Ghost Dance that upset the settlers

in Visalia and over Redwood Saddle
to graze Rowell and Sugarloaf bunchgrass.
After nearly a hundred summers,

the cows knew the way.
It's much the same once off the trail:
pine needle carpets and granite cut

by snowmelt creeks and green stringer
meadow, wind and river talking loud
enough to hear damn-near anything.

By the Spring By the River

By Buck Ramsey
(1938-1998)

Not Heifetz
By Don Weller

The fall down
Scanty on the scattered trees
Lighted in their color
Our way to the endline camp.
No one could know,
I did not and you did not,
What on earth we had in store there.
Blessed as we were,
We went blind but for the lighted leaves
Merely hoping for something like a light hello.
Then up jumped a fiddle
And a frozen old guitar
Missing in the middle
The crucial D.
Midst talk of cattle and trails plowed under
And men out of the old rock who had ground back to dirt,
I saw my part, the part I would play.
I thought to strike a D note in my head
To hum when it came my part to play
Back there behind the tunes as Freddie fiddled
For Wildwood Annie as she sailed Over the Waves
At Three O'clock in the Morning
With the Wednesday Night Waltz.
The D, you see, became me and I was the D and so much little more
As the thawed old guitar went its own way
To play its orchestral part
For the soaring obbligatos
Of the fiddle by Freddie's cheek
I thought to myself
As all of you played your parts so well,
As we filled in with the stars,
As I hummed in now and then with my simple D,
That this is the true way you put things together.

Boomer Johnson

By Henry Herbert Knibbs (1874-1945)

Now Mr. Boomer Johnson was a gettin' old in spots,
But you don't expect a bad man to go wrastlin' pans and pots;
But he'd done his share of killin' and his draw was gettin' slow,
So he quits a-punchin' cattle and he takes to punchin' dough.

Our foreman up and hires him, figurin' age had rode him tame,
But a snake don't get no sweeter just by changin' of its name.
Well, Old Boomer knowed his business—he could cook to make you smile,
But say, he wrangled fodder in a most peculiar style.

After a Rainy Night
By James Boren
(1925-2010)

He never used no matches—left 'em layin' on the shelf,
Just some kerosene and cussin' and the kindlin' lit itself.
And, pardner, I'm allowin' it would give a man a jolt
To see him stir frijoles with the barrel of his Colt.

Now killin' folks and cookin' ain't so awful far apart,
That musta been why Boomer kept a-practicin' his art;
With the front sight of his pistol he would cut a pie lid slick,
And he'd crimp her with the muzzle for to make the edges stick.

He built his doughnuts solid, and it sure would curl your hair
To see him plug a doughnut as he tossed it in the air.
He bored the holes plum center every time his pistol spoke,
Till the can was full of doughnuts and the shack was full of smoke.

We-all was gettin' jumpy, but he couldn't understand
Why his shootin' made us nervous when his cookin' was so grand.
He kept right on performin', and it weren't no big surprise
When he took to markin' tombstones on the covers of his pies.

They didn't taste no better and they didn't taste no worse,
But a-settin' at the table was like ridin' in a hearse;
You didn't do no talkin' and you took just what you got,
So we et till we was foundered just to keep from gettin' shot.

When at breakfast one bright mornin', I was feelin' kind of low,
Old Boomer passed the doughnuts and I tells him plenty: "No.
All I takes this trip is coffee, for my stomach is a wreck."
I could see the itch for killin' swell the wattle on his neck.

Scorn his grub? He strings some doughnuts on the muzzle of his gun,
And he shoves her in my gizzard and he says, "You're takin' one!"
He was set to start a graveyard, but for once he was mistook;
Me not wantin' any doughnuts, I just up and salts the cook.

Did they fire him? Listen, pardner, there was nothin' left to fire,
Just a row of smilin' faces and another cook to hire.
If he joined some other outfit and is cookin', what I mean,
It's where they ain't no matches and they don't need kerosene.

A Bolt of Broomtails
By Rod Miller

Across alkali flat and sandhill,
Over the sage-covered plain
The mesteñada flows like fabric,
Dancing ahead of its dusty train.

chestnut, claybank,
coyote dun,
buckskin, black,
blue roan, bay,
piebald, palomino,
pinto, paint,
grulla, ghost white,
dapple gray

Rippling in the morning light
The hues shimmer and shift;
Mustangs run as colored threads
Through the warp and weft.

The Hawk and the Hay Field

By Lisa Quinlan

"Ah, there you are, I was looking for you."
I watch him circle and hover over the windrower,
Waiting for a frightened mouse or rabbit
To run out of its disappearing cover.
I slow down and reach for my camera,
But when I look up
He is halfway across the field
Sitting on a cut row of hay.
He watches me go back and forth a couple of times,
Flies up,
Then swoops to catch a mouse in his perfected claws.
He sits there a while before his powerful wings
Take him out of sight.
He will come back and do it all over again.
This time he hovers long enough
For two clicks of the camera.

The shadows grow longer and darker now.
He comes back one last time.
He's closer to the windrower than he has been all day,
Hovering low, even with the window.
I stop and reach for my camera
And a good close-up shot.
I notice him looking straight at me
As if he were saying
"Thanks, see you next time."
My hand levitates into a wave and I say
"Yea. See you next time."
Then he gently flies away.
Just, flies away.

**Harris Hawk at
the Rabbit Ranch**
By Thomas Quinn

From Town

By Badger Clark (1883-1957)

We're the children of the open and we hate the haunts o' men
But we had to come to town to get the mail.
And we're ridin' home at daybreak—'cause the air is cooler then—
All 'cept one of us that stopped behind in jail.
Shorty's nose won't bear paradin', Bill's off eye is darkly fadin',
All our toilets show a touch of disarray,
For we found that City life is a constant round of strife
And we ain't the breed for shyin' from a fray.

Chant your warhoops, pardners, dear, while the east turns pale with fear
And the chaparral is tremblin' all aroun'
For we're wicked to the marrer; we're a midnight dream of terror
When we're ridin' up the rocky trail from town!

We acquired our hasty temper from our friend, the centipede.
From the rattlesnake we learned to guard our rights.
We have gathered fightin' pointers from the famous bronco steed
And the bobcat teached us repertee that bites.
So when some high-collared herrin' jeered the garb that I was wearin'
'Twasn't long till we had got where talkin' ends,
And he et his ill-bred chat, with a sauce of derby hat,
While my merry pardners entertained his friends.

Sing 'er out, my buckeroos! Let the desert hear the news.
Tell the stars the way we rubbed the haughty down.
We're the fiercest wolves a-prowlin' and it's just our night for howlin'
When we're ridin' up the rocky trail from town.

Since the days that Lot and Abram split the Jordan range in halves,
Just to fix it so their punchers wouldn't fight,
Since old Jacob skinned his dad-in-law of six years' crop of calves
And then hit the trail for Canaan in the night,
There has been a taste for battle 'mong the men that follow cattle
And a love of doin' things that's wild and strange,
And the warmth of Laban's words when he missed his speckled herds
Still is useful in the language of the range.

Sing 'er out, my bold coyotes! leather fists and leather throats,
For we wear the brand of Ishm'el like a crown.
We're the sons of desolation, we're the outlaws of creation—
E-Yow! a-ridin' up the rocky trail from town.

"Eating is an agricultural act."

WENDELL BERRY, "WHAT ARE PEOPLE FOR"

We Rode Out on the Morning
By Gary Morton

Beach Ride
By Jim Wodark

Ah, Pacifica!
By Virginia Bennett

Three branches, heavily laden with velvet moss,
arbored over the two-laned paved road
like an entrance to some Hobbit-filled sanctuary,
where a myriad of magical streams flowed.

Every bit of vegetation looked eerily strange
and unfamiliar as a platypus clone
to a cowboy in search of a glimpse of the ocean,
comfortable only in sagebrush and piñon.

Twenty calving seasons had passed since he'd seen it,
tho' he longed for it deep in his heart.
And, now, between ranch jobs, only one day's drive away
toward the sea, this land-locked sailor set his chart.

He drove 'til he found an inviting beach, then
down the sawgrass lined path, he hit a lope.
And because of warning, regulatory signs,
his heeler trotted with him at the end of a rope.

To some, it might not have been the perfect day,
broiling in over the waves came a thick fog.
But, in wonderment and awe, the cowboy knelt down…
and pointed out the ocean to his dog.

He took no notice that the tourists stopped to stare
at his head-topping Stetson, black and grand.
He just whistled to his cowdog and headed down the spit,
leaving incongruous boot-tracks in the sand.

As You Ride
By Virginia Bennett

As you ride the high sierras
with your packstring and your pony
and your heart beats strong and lonely,
as the waves upon the sea,
does that eerie pull which drew us
into this moth-like dance,
cause your musings 'neath the moonrise
to ever stop and think of me?

Do you ever take my picture
from your saddlebag of mem'ries,
hold it backlit by the campfire,
view its facets in the flame?
And when the coyotes' music
rings out over lonesome ridges
on a starry eve, I wonder,
do they ever sing my name?

When the breezes comb the treetops
of a spruce and aspen forest,
and the stones of unforgotten longing
make you toss upon your bed,
do you lie awake and listen
to wind sweeping through the valley
wishing you could somehow capture
whispered words of what I've said?

I will watch, with glances lingering,
the rimrock trail above my cabin,
and strain to see your silhouette
against a twilight sky.
I will bide, in expectation,
to hear your bit-chains jingling,
and hope to soon see northern lights
reflected in your horse's eye.

Longtime Cowgirl
By Nancy Boren

Snickers
By William Matthews

The Staff of Life

By Linda Hussa

One of the buckaroos
high-graded
a jug of wine
and brought it into camp.
He filled everybody's cup.
He handed one to
Billy McCluskey.

Billy took a big swig
and shuddered,

"Coffee's the staff of life…
but this is better."

Spoken by Pete Crystal

A Trailside Boulder Story

By Joel Nelson

A thick fog shrouded boulder piles as darkness turned to day
Giving juniper and piñon pines a scattered look as they
Drifted softly out to meet him in the chilly quiet morn
And the short rope that he packed that day was tied fast to the horn
The horse he'd been reserving had hard black unshod feet
For the sound of horseshoe meeting rock would be too indiscreet—
Might warn this last old mossyhorn and tip the puncher's hand
Might blow the weeks of scouting and the ambush he had planned.
For the first damp day and foggy after days of dusty trails
When the powdered paths—now damp on top—would amplify the tales
Of hoofprints cloven—minutes old—and glaring in the mist
Laid down covertly by the steer that somehow had been missed.
For years by gay and laughing hands with tie strings on their chaps
Who might as well have stayed in camp on cook and hoodie's laps
As to ride outside a crackin' jokes and telegraphin' notes
On cool crisp mountain mornings when every pin drop floats
Up to the haunts of this old steer who'd listen all the while
As the crew below tossed coffee cups and tin plates in a pile
Who stood with ease a trembling—sculpture standing still
He was cagey as a mule deer buck, this steer that owned the hill
He'd been taught his lesson early and he picked up on it quick
That one time he'd been gathered and the smoke and dust grew thick
And nylon tightened round his heels and after he'd been thrown
The sting of iron and cutting knife, and the blood smell was his own
He'd somehow lost his mother when the holocaust was ended
And he'd quit the bunch just runnin' blind—he'd run till he was winded
And running blind in terror letting instinct give direction
He had somehow hit a pocket that was hidden from detection.
And this had been his background behind mountain laurel hedges
That never lost their leaves in fall and the path into them wedges
Under slanted sandstone overhangs above a slickrock trail
That will not show a hoofprint or give away the tale
Of the steer that makes his bed there and soaks up sun by day
Where the laurel blossom's fragrant from March to early May
Where he's sheltered from the northers and the heat of summer sun
Where the punchers blithely pass in pairs the entry to his run
Where he's lived to reach these golden years by grazing out at night
When there's small chance for detection or unnecessary flight.
Now two good years of seeping springs and timely summer rain
And bumper crops of grama grass have put a heavy gain
On every bovine critter with our mossyhorn included
Till his hide was stretched to bustin' and his old sides had protruded
To the point they rub the sandstone along the trailside wall
And leave a smoothly polished rub at the entry to his hall.
Well a camp man's life can lonely be between the roundup seasons

Ol' Cranky
By Vel Miller

For its solo work a horseback and he's always huntin' reasons
To push himself a ways beyond the limits set by most
On what one man can do alone, and so, let's raise a toast
To the camp man prowlin' all alone who happened by the place
Where the mossyhorn would quit the trail and leave no sign or trace
Except that little polished streak there on the smooth rock wall
The puncher's memory told him that it wasn't there last fall.
This led to days of checking trails and hoofprints shape and size
For the camp man's friend was time itself and he could strategize
On just the kind of place and day when odds were with the man
This takes us back to barefoot horse and foggy morning plan.
The cowboy made a circle 'cross the cattle trails he's learned,
And the damp unbroken trail dust said the steer had not returned
But would be coming shortly from this morning's water hole
The entry to his hideaway was now blocked with a pole
That turned the steer a little so the cowboy had a shot
From behind a trailside boulder—and one loop's all he's got
But one was all he needed with an underhanded throw
The big steer's holler echoed through the canyons down below.
Then the puncher tied him to an oak—and let me tell you pard
It wasn't all that easy—but it wasn't all that hard
Just a cowboy working solo on some ranch someplace out west
Just an ordinary camp man—not the worst and not the best.
Oh! The cowboy drug away the pole and rolled it off a bluff
It had somehow served its purpose and the steer was proof enough
Then he left his ground-tied barefoot horse and slipped back to the tree
With knife in hand and one smooth cut he set the old steer free.
And I 'spect the old steer still beds down where mountain laurels grow
And I 'spect he drinks by starlight at the water hole below
And I'll bet he stops and listens and sniffs the air for sign
At the boulder by the trailside where the puncher threw his twine
And now the years have rolled by—a half a score or more
And mornings now the laughing waddies ride out as before
And at least one steer stands sentinel and sniffs the frosty air
And hearing waddies down below he slips into his lair
But if by chance they happen by the polished sandstone wall
Their eyes are drawn the other way by a name they all recall
Carved in the trunk of that sturdy oak that served as snubbing tree
The name they know—the year he left—and "Pasó Por Aquí"!

*"When cattle, for one reason or another, are born or become wild
in big country where they might only water every other day, a story like
this one could take place."—Joel Nelson*
Note: "Hoodie" is a cowboy word for hoodlum, aka cook's helper.

That Spotted Sow

By Carlos Ashley (1904–1993)

Did you ever hear the story
    Of that famous hog of mine?
She's a razorback and spotted
    Black and white from hoof to spine;

With a snout made outa granite,
    She can root just like a plow;
And the fence ain't been invented
    That can turn that spotted sow.

Born and bred on Cedar Mountain,
    She is wilder than a deer;
And she's known by reputation
    To the ranch hands far and near.

Though a sow of mine had raised 'er,
    On that mountain she was free;
And I always kinda doubted
    That she really b'longed to me.

She didn't claim no owner—
    Save the God who put 'er there—
And for moral man's relations
    She just simply didn't care.

She preferred the solemn silence
    Of her Cedar Mountain home,
And most of all she wanted us
    To let 'er plum alone.

The Spotted Sow
By Cheri Christensen

Ever' Fall I'd try to mark 'er,
    But she'd get away agin;
And I reckon that my cussin',
    Though artistic, was a sin.

Well, I sold my brand in '30—
    Moved out ever' hog an' cow;
Rounded up…yeah…all but one head,
    All but that blamed spotted sow.

So we organized against 'er—
    Got the best of dogs and men;
But we never got good started
    Puttin' that hog in a pen.

Now we really went a-huntin'
    When we tried to catch Ole Spot;
We left the ranch at daylight
    And her trail was always hot.

She might be pickin' acorns
    On the banks of Sandy Creek,
Or in somebody's turnips
    Cultivatin', so to speak.

But let the foot of dog or man
    Disturb the morning dew,
And you might as well a phoned 'er,
    'Cause, somehow, she always knew.

She'd light out for Cedar Mountain,
    Where the land and sky divide—
There ain't no spot on earth nowhere
    A better place to hide.

We'd hear the pack a-bayin'
    Up the mountain loud and clear,
But before we rode up to 'em
    That ole sow would disappear.

Or she'd rally 'gainst a boulder,
    Bristlin' like a porcupine,
Till a dog forgot his caution—
    Then she'd cut him into twine.

Killin' dogs was just a pastime
    To that hog; I'm tellin' you,
With them long, curved, knifelike tuches
    She could slice a houn' in two.

She could whip most any critter
    On four legs I ever saw,
And she had a perfect record
    'Cause she never fought a draw.

Now the more I tried to catch 'er,
    And the more I give it thought,
I begin to get the notion
    She's opposed to bein' caught.

I couldn't help admire that sow,
    When all was done and said;
For, to tell the truth about 'er,
    She was really thoroughbred.

She had character and courage
    And the heart to do the right;
And when it come to fightin',
    Now she shore as hell could fight.

Well, the Fall froze into Winter,
    And the Winter thawed to Spring
April watered hill and valley;
    Maytime painted ever'thing.

Late one evenin' just at sundown
    I was ridin' home right slow,
When I passed a lonesome water hole
    And saw…it was a show.

Ole Spot was trailin' down the hill
    And right behind her trotted
Ten baby pigs not ten days old,
    And ever'one was spotted.

Tailend
By Cheri Christensen

Western Heritage
By Jason Rich

What Will I Tell Him?

By Waddie Mitchell

What will I tell him, you ask me,
When my son's trying to make up his mind
To ride for a living like I have
Or explore what the world has to find.
Could I tell him it's sure worth the doing?
Could I tell him I spent well my time?
I'll just say from the start,
Son, it's gotta come from the heart,
It ain't something that comes from the mind.
I'll tell him the truth as I know it—
Of good years, hard winters, and drought.
The ecstasy of winnin' a round now and then
Givin' courage to stay in the bout.
That adrenaline rush when you're bustin' up brush
On a cowpony agile and stout,
Of having the rug jerked from under your feet
When you hear that the outfit sold out.
I'll tell him that cowboy's a verb, not a noun;
It's what you do more than a name.
And he'd be foolin' himself if he's figurin'
On any sort of material gain.
I'll remind him of spring calves a buckin',
Of the joy and the pride and the pain
Of livin' a life that is easy or hard
At the discretion of nature's refrain.
What will I tell him, you ask me,
When he's there and tryin' to make up his mind?
I'll just say from the start,
Son, it's gotta come from the heart,
It ain't something that comes from the mind.

Waddie
By William Matthews

"When I was 16," Waddie remembers, "I just didn't think I was needin' school anymore. When my boy was gonna turn 16, I was asked, 'What are you gonna tell him if he comes up to you and says that he's just gonna quit school, just go cowboy for a living?' So I thought about that."

Sandhills Spring
By Jim Rey

Waiting for Daylight

By John Dofflemyer

No alarm clock here, we take turns
waking up on the hour before the first
branding of the year, lists of implements,

food and vaccines checked in our sleep
before heading up the hill, leaving
convenience for the make-do miles

off the asphalt where anything can happen
despite best-laid plans. We should be
too old, too accustomed to this drill

to toss and turn—we should be sure
and secure with familiar faces and horses,
good hands and neighbors come to help,

like always. Grown old together, we
understand what we have lost—yet shake
out another loop just to grin into the sun.

With the Cattle

By Banjo Paterson (1864-1941)

The drought is down on field and flock,
    The river bed is dry;
And we must shift the starving stock
    Before the cattle die.
We muster up with weary hearts
    At breaking of the day,
And turn our heads to foreign parts,
    To take the stock away.
        And it's hunt 'em up and dog 'em,
        And it's get the whip and flog 'em,
For it's weary work is droving when they're
    dying every day;
        By stock routes bare and eaten,
        On dusty roads and beaten,
With half a chance to save their lives we
    take the stock away.

We cannot use the whip for shame
    On beasts that crawl along;
We have to drop the weak and lame,
    And try to save the strong;
The wrath of God is on the track.
    The drought fiend holds his sway,
With blows and cries and stockwhip crack
    We take the stock away.
        As they fall we leave them lying,
        With the crows to watch them dying,
Grim sextons of the Overland that fasten on their prey:
        By the fiery dust storm drifting,
        And the mocking mirage shifting,
In heat and drought and hopeless pain we
    take the stock away.

In dull despair the days go by
    With never hope of change,
But every stage we draw more nigh
    Towards the mountain range;
And some may live to climb the pass,
    And reach the great plateau,
And revel in the mountain grass,
    By streamlets fed with snow.
        As the mountain wind is blowing
        It starts the cattle lowing,
And calling to each other down the dusty long array;

And there speaks a grizzled drover:
    "Well, thank God, the worst is over,
The creatures smell the mountain grass that's
    twenty miles away."

They press towards the mountain grass,
    They look with eager eyes
Along the rugged stony pass,
    That slopes towards the skies;
Their feet may bleed from rocks and stones,
    But though the blood-drop starts,
They struggle on with stifled groans,
    For hope is in their hearts.
        And the cattle that are leading,
        Though their feet are worn and bleeding,
Are breaking to a kind of run—pull up, and let them go!
        For the mountain wind is blowing,
        And the mountain grass is growing,
They settle down by running streams
    ice-cold with melted snow.

The days are done of heat and drought
    Upon the stricken plain;
The wind has shifted right about,
    And brought the welcome rain;
The river runs with sullen roar,
    All flecked with yellow foam,
And we must take the road once more,
    To bring the cattle home.
        And it's "Lads! we'll raise a chorus,
        There's a pleasant trip before us."
And the horses bound beneath us as we start
    them down the track;
        And the drovers canter, singing,
        Through the sweet green grasses springing,
Towards the far-off mountain land,
    to bring the cattle back.

Are these the beasts we brought away
    That move so lively now?
They scatter off like flying spray
    Across the mountain's brow;
And dashing down the rugged range
    We hear the stockwhip crack,

Bringing 'Em Home
By S.C. Mummert

Good faith, it is a welcome change
   To bring such cattle back.
      And it's "Steady down the lead there!"
      And it's "Let 'em stop and feed there!"
For they're wild as mountain eagles and
   their sides are all afoam;
      But they're settling down already,
      And they'll travel nice and steady,
With cheery call and jest and song we fetch
      the cattle home.

We have to watch them close at night
   For fear they'll make a rush,
And break away in headlong flight
   Across the open bush;
And by the campfire's cheery blaze,
   With mellow voice and strong,
We hear the lonely watchman raise
   The Overlander's song:
      "Oh! it's when we're done with roving.
      With the camping and the droving,

It's homeward down the Bland we'll go,
   and never more we'll roam";
      While the stars shine out above us,
      Like the eyes of those who love us—
The eyes of those who watch and wait to greet
      the cattle home.

The plains are all awave with grass,
   The skies are deepest blue;
And leisurely the cattle pass
   And feed the long day through;
But when we sight the station gate,
   We make the stockwhips crack,
A welcome sound to those who wait
   To greet the cattle back:
      And through the twilight falling
      We hear their voices calling,
As the cattle splash across the ford and
   churn it into foam;
      And the children run to meet us,
      And our wives and sweethearts greet us,
Their heroes from the Overland who brought
      the cattle home.

Windmill Juice
By Mary Ross Buchholz

The Pearl of Them All

By William Henry Ogilvie
(1869-1963)

Gaily in front of the stockwhip
The horses come galloping home,
Leaping and bucking and playing
With sides all a lather of foam;
But painfully, slowly behind them,
With head to the crack of the fall,
And trying so gamely to follow
Comes limping the pearl of them all.

He is stumbling and stiff in the shoulder,
And splints from the hoof to the knee,
But never a horse on the station
Has half such a spirit as he;
Give these all the boast of their breeding
These pets of the paddock and stall,
But ten years ago not their proudest
Could live with the pearl of them all.

No journey has ever yet beat him,
No day was too heavy or hard,
He was king of the camp and the muster
And pride of the wings of the yard;
But Time is relentless to follow;
The best of us bow to his thrall;
And death, with his scythe on his shoulder,
Is dogging the pearl of them all.

I watch him go whinnying past me,
And memories come with a whirl
Of reckless, wild rides with a comrade
And laughing, gay rides with a girl—
How she decked him with lilies and love-knots
And plaited his mane at my side,
And once in the grief of a parting
She threw her arms round him and cried.

And I promised—I gave her my promise
The night that we parted in tears,
To keep and be kind to the old horse
Till Time made a burden of years;
And then for his sake and one woman's…
So, fetch me my gun from the wall!
I have only this kindness to offer
As gift to the pearl of them all.

Break Time
By Mary Ross Buchholz

Here! hold him out there by the yard wing,
And don't let him know by a sign:
Turn his head to you—ever so little!
I can't bear his eyes to meet mine.
Then—stand still, old boy! for a moment…
These tears, how they blind as they fall!
Now, God help my hand to be steady…
Goodbye!—to the pearl of them all!

Talking Horses

By Jim Sagel
(1947-1998)

uncle steven rolls his own
as we sit in the last sun
    under skeletal alamos
and talk horses

how his bitch of a mare
throws everyone except him
even if he is seventy-nine
    he's broken green horses
ribs collarbones and legs
nearly long as he can remember
never misses the horse races
    at Alcalde
where he bets half his social
    security check
on his mean-eyed appaloosa
and almost never wins

uncle flicks the butt
into the muddy ditch
and snorts a laugh remembering
the time the movie company
hired half of San Juan
as extras in a john wayne movie
    a couple of years back
and the director brought in
a show-off hollywood 12 gallon hatted
    stunt man
to teach the "*natives*" how to ride
who
first day out
got thrown on his ass
    right in front of the Indians
and the director got pissed
because they had to stop filming
    that day
since no one could stop laughing

uncle steven and me
just sitting
smoking
and talking horses

been at it for years now
but he's never once mentioned
the horse
that reared and trampled his boy

**When Attention Changes
From the Ride to the Landing**
By Don Weller

A Cowboy's Christmas Prayer

By S. Omar Barker

(1894-1985)

I ain't much good at prayin',
    and You may not know me, Lord—
I ain't much seen in churches
    where they preach Thy Holy Word,
But You may have observed me
    out here on the lonely plains,
A-lookin' after cattle,
    feelin' thankful when it rains,

Admirin' Thy great handiwork,
    the miracle of grass,
Aware of Thy kind spirit
    in the way it comes to pass
That hired men on horseback
    and the livestock that we tend
Can look up at the stars at night
    and know we've got a Friend.

So here's ol' Christmas comin' on,
    remindin' us again
Of Him whose coming brought goodwill
    into the hearts of men.
A cowboy ain't a preacher, Lord,
    but if You'll hear my prayer,
I'll ask as good as we have got
    for all men everywhere.

Don't let no hearts be bitter, Lord.
    Don't let no child be cold.
Make easy beds for them that's sick
    and them that's weak and old.
Let kindness bless the trail we ride,
    no matter what we're after,
And sorter keep us on Your side,
    in tears as well as laughter.

I've seen ol' cows a-starvin',
    and it ain't no happy sight:
Please don't leave no one hungry, Lord,
    on Thy good Christmas night—
No man, no child, no woman,
    and no critter on four feet

We've Got Mail
By Jim Rey

I'll do my doggone best
    to help you find 'em chuck to eat.

I'm just a sinful cowpoke, Lord—
    ain't got no business prayin'
But still I hope You'll ketch a word
    or two of what I'm sayin':
We speak of Merry Christmas, Lord—
    I reckon You'll agree—

There ain't no Merry Christmas
    for nobody that ain't free!
So one thing more I'll ask You,
    Lord: just help us what You can
To save some seeds of freedom
    for the future sons of man!

Lunging a Filly

By Katie Andraski

As I swiveled behind my coming yearling
I watched how she eased around me
Like water over cobbles.
She flowed away from me like I was a hill.

Until she ducked her head and slammed
Against the line, splashing kicks.
Young to submission and full of joy
She played. Then dropped her crest.

Private Conversation

By Ann Hanson

The Tyrants
By Thomas Quinn

A Winter Morning
By Ted Kooser

A farmhouse window far back from the highway
speaks to the darkness in a small, sure voice.
Against this stillness, only a kettle's whisper,
and against the starry cold, one small blue ring of flame.

Sheepherder

By Linda Hussa

Basco boy, you
    left your sheep bedded
    walked the many ridges
    through a dark where lightning warned you back

    to stand outside the homesteader cabin in the rain
    until he found you
    took you inside where you sat on the floor
    shivering
    and watched the young girl they called teacher
    move like a dance

    and speak to his children in their language
    you didn't understand

    but her voice was enough.

    The man put you out at last
    closed the door on her eyes.

    You found the flock still bedded near your dogs

    and for days
    and nights
    you heard her voice say,
    "Good night,
            basco boy."

From "Where the Wind Lives"

Evening Visitors
By Jim Wodark

Rockin' J Cowgirls
By Nancy Boren

Companions

By Joan Shaddox Isom

When Old Age raps on my window and beckons
with bony finger, I'll not follow her
behind closed shutters to measure out my life
with nose drops at 2:00 pm, a teaspoon of tonic
before Lawrence Welk, No...

I will tell her to come with me
and I will take her on the handlebars of my bicycle
and whizz her through the streets,
both of us in blue jeans, our hair quite gray,
and they will say,
"Look at those two old ladies!
They don't know how to grow old with dignity!"

So, maybe we'll stop by for Dignity,
pull her protesting, to the park,
strip off her rolled-down hose,
show her how to run barefoot, fly kites,
pet mangy dogs
and rouge her mouth with red popsicles.

We'll tie a bright balloon to the handlebars
as we ride home at dusk, singing a bawdy song,
and Dignity, still drunk from the Ferris wheel,
her hat askew, will wave a wistful goodbye
as we careen around the corner, Old Age and I,
giving one last exuberant cry.

From "The Moon in Five Disguises"

Hat Dance
By Buckeye Blake

Between Brandings

By Carolyn Dufurrena

Ibuprofen and Early Times,
A frozen slab of home-cured bacon
Wrapped in a clean white T-shirt
Tucked in the hollow of your back
Dulls the knife
Wedged between your lumbar vertebrae.

Not like cortisone,
Not like surgery.
Not going to town for awhile.

Bog Hot Meadow/First Pass

By Carolyn Dufurrena

Silence cocoons the morning
Stretches the horizon
Snow on ridges
Blue with distance
Coiling ribbon of dust
Across the valley:
An invisible traveler
Trundling to town.

The ticking of grass growing
Marks the ripening day.

Finally,
A ripple in the wavering distance,
A russet ribbon of motion
slips in and out of view,
As though parting the silent universe between earth and sky.

Shimmer resolves to form:
Horses
Moving fast across the curve of earth,
Parsing the soundless space
Between sage and greasewood.
Their flashing legs
Dance an invisible trail
Up the desert.

They blow by thundering,
Pounding the earth,
Stretched full out across the short salt
    grass of meadow.

Lead mare pulls up short.
She turns.
The rest swing with her.

Step, step.
A careful trot.
Wait.

They see it.
They know what day this is.
Necks stretch low,
Tails flick,
Whickering
To their foals
As they decide
Whether
To accept the gate,

The journey into summer.

**The Art of Running
Through the Sage**
By Karen G. Myers

The Time to Decide

By Bruce Kiskaddon

(1878-1950)

Did you ever stand on the ledges,
On the brink of the great plateau
And look from their jagged edges
On the country that lay below?

When your vision met no resistance
And nothing to stop your gaze,
Till the mountain peaks in the distance
Stood wrapped in a purple haze.

On the winding watercourses
And the trails on the mountainsides,
Where you guided your patient horses
On your long and lonesome rides.

When you saw Earth's open pages
And you seemed to understand
As you gazed on the work of ages,
Rugged and rough, but grand.

There, the things that you thought were strongest
And the things that you thought were great,
And for which you had striven longest
Seemed to carry but little weight.

While the things that were always nearer,
The things that you thought were small;
Seemed to stand out grander and clearer
As you looked from the mountain wall.

While you're gazing on such a vision
And your outlook is clear and wide,
If you have to make a decision,
That's the time and place to decide.

Although you return to the city
And mingle again with the throng;
Though your heart may be softened by pity
Or bitter from strife and wrong.

Though others should laugh in derision,
And the voice of the past grow dim;
Yet, stick to the cool decision
That you made on the mountain's rim.

The Cowhunter
By Jim Rey

Fixing the Spring

By Carolyn Dufurrena

High in a granite notch
an avalanche of wild roses
hides the springbox.

I balance on sharp boulders
poking up between hummocks in the bog,

look down into my reflection
in still black water.

Compressor chuffing,
he hollers from below,
"See anything yet?"

Nothing yet, I say,
but then
a messy braid of roots flashes in the icy water,
just for a moment,
snaking back and forth, down in the cold dark.

I reach in and pull: like
trying to yank Ophelia
out of the depths.

She holds tight. I lean back.
My boots teeter on the boulders,
islands in a sluggish stream.

The long braid loosens,
comes all at once
a six-foot serpent of roots pulled free,
and the freezing water roils,
rises in a three-foot column over the lip
of the pipe, the earth releasing
its long, dark watery breath,

boils, black and icy,
over boots, jeans, boulders
to run clear and sparkling
and full again,
feeding the pipeline, the troughs far below,
feeding livestock, antelope, deer,
feeding sage grouse, magpies,
renewing this most precious gift:
water in a dry land.

Magpies Moved
By Thomas Quinn

Into the Drift
By William Matthews

To the Thawing Wind

By Robert Frost (1874-1963)

Come with rain, O loud Southwester!
Bring the singer, bring the nester;
Give the buried flower a dream;
Make the settled snowbank steam;
Find the brown beneath the white;
But whate'er you do tonight,
Bathe my window, make it flow,
Melt it as the ice will go;
Melt the glass and leave the sticks
Like a hermit's crucifix;
Burst into my narrow stall;
Swing the picture on the wall;
Run the rattling pages o'er;
Scatter poems on the floor;
Turn the poet out of door.

A Sure Sign of Winter
By Tom Browning

The Men of Open Spaces

**By William Henry Ogilvie
(1869-1963)**

These are the men with the sun-tanned faces
and the keen far-sighted eyes—
the men of the open spaces,
and the land where the mirage lies.

The men who have learnt to master
the forces of fire and drought
and the demon Flood's disaster in
the fields of furthest out.

The men who have stood together
and shared in the fight with fate
and known the strength of the tether
that holds a mate to his mate.

Who ride with a gallant bearing
where every saddle's a throne,
and each is an emperor sharing
an empire enough for his own.

They are strangers to airs and graces,
and scornful of power and pride—
the Men of the Open Spaces,
who rule the world when they ride.

*Born in Scotland, Will Ogilvie lived in Australia for a dozen years,
where he became a top station hand, drover and horse breaker.*

Down the River

By Henry Lawson (1867-1922)

I've done with joys and misery
    An' why should I repine?
There's no one knows the past but me
    An' that ol' dog o' mine.
We camp an' walk, an' camp an' walk,
    An' find it fairly good;
He can do anything but talk—
    An' wouldn't if he could.

We sits an' thinks beside the fire,
    With all the stars a-shine
An' no one knows our thoughts but me
    An' that there dog o' mine

We has our johnny-cake an' scrag
    An' finds 'em fairly good;
He can do anything but talk—
    An' wouldn't, if he could.

I has my smoke, he has his rest,
    When sunset's getting dim;
An' if I do get drunk at times,
    It's all the same to him.
So long's he's got my swag to mind,
    He thinks that times is good;
He can do anything but talk—
    An' wouldn't, if he could.

Trio in Black and White
By Don Weller

All I Want

By Luci Tapahonso

All I want is the bread to turn out like hers just once
          brown crust
          soft, airy insides
          rich and round
that is all.
So I ask her: How many cups?
          Ah yaa ah, she says,
          tossing flour and salt into a large silver bowl.
          I don't measure with cups.
          I just know by my hands,
          just a little like this is right, see?
          You young people always ask
          those kinds of questions,
          she says,
thrusting her arms into the dough
and turning it over and over again.
The table trembles with her movements.
I watch silently and this coffee is good,
                    strong and fresh.
          Outside, her son is chopping wood,
          his body an intense arc.
          The dull rhythm of winter
          is the swinging of the axe
          and the noise of children squeezing in
          with the small sighs of wind
          through the edges of the windows.

She pats and tosses it furiously
shaping balls of warm, soft dough.
          There, we'll let it rise,
          she says, sitting down now.
          We drink coffee and there is nothing
          like the warm smell of bread rising
          on windy, woodchopping afternoons.

The Slipper Waltz

By Buck Ramsey

(1938-1998)

I   The Meeting

Kid Tybo Tremain of the old Star Cross outfit
Had yet his last measure to grow,
But he rode like a tick on brush country cow dog
And looped the beast, head, heel or toe.

But Kid wasn't quite yet that dashing young cowboy
We hear of in story or song,
For just drawing nigh to the calico faction
Made all he did right come out wrong.

Each grin he got off bore the tick of a felon
Caught lurking where there was a theft,
His circuits were switched on so his gaze came out
    cross-eyed
And everything right came out left.

The lotions and oils he spread on for improvement
Seemed extracts of skunkberry brush,
And just a few swigs from straight sasparilla
Made Kid lurch around like a lush.

So he'd as soon stay with his bunkhouse beguilements
And rifle his dofunny file
When Fiddle and Fair rode the rough outside circle
Of scuffles and wooing and wile.

But dreams will bring notions that bother young
    cowboys
One season when they are a teen,
When all the critters that live all around
Are aroused by the air of a spring.

So once he nerved-up and he rode the wide circle
Determined to act his sixteen,
And there, oh, there by a twining vine bower
Was something he'd never dare dream.

She seemed to the Kid near the size of an angel;
She had eyes, and about her were ways.
In all, there was something, the vision of something
That stayed with all of his days.

His look ever followed her, though at a distance,
And soon hers and his found a meeting.
They both looked away, looked away, looked away,
But sure with each look was a reading.

For Tybo's eyes only, she misplaced her slippers
When time changed from dancing to riding,
And sometime between then and when all had departed
Those slippers were taken from hiding.

The Kid announced one day his regular prowling
Might take him a few extra hours,
For he had discovered the home whereabout
Of the vision he had by the bowers.

To understand all of the dire intonations
That came of this first fretful meeting
Would take in the telling a leisure much longer
Than waiting the bloom from the seeding.

II   The Visit

So yes, Tybo trembled at facing the wonder,
But worried much more that he'd face her just once,
For he knew one visit must bring on another
Or she'd be forgetting this cowboy for months.

So he took one slipper from out of his saddlebag,
Starched up his will and walked up to her door.
He shuffled around, said he forgot the other
And reckoned he'd just have to make one ride more.

"And I got to thinkin' while ridin' to your place,"
He blushed and was feeling bowlegs go knock-kneed—
"No disrespect—I wish for wearin' the slippers
That you…were fixed 'bout…like…a she centipede."

I know you are laughing and think this is silly.
Poor Cupid plumb blushed being this kid's envoy.
But Kid learned to laugh, learned to dance with a lady,
And soon he'd be known as a dashing cowboy.

Rim Rock Romance
By Buckeye Blake

> "Cattle die, kinsmen die,
> the self must also die;
> I know one thing which never dies:
> the reputation of each dead man."

12TH CENTURY ICELANDIC FROM
"SAYINGS OF THE HIGH ONE (HÁVAMÁL)"

Grist

By J.B. Allen
(1938-2005)

There's a place back in them hills
That's sorta hid and hard to find
Where a spring of crystal water
Leaves the rock and starts to wind
Down amongst the rocks and brambles
To the river—miles away
And beside it stands a cabin
Where the chipmunks come to play.

Far from worldly lines of commerce
Tucked away from fellow men
A hardy soul had stopped a spell
To sink some roots and then
Succumbed to sudden illness—
So the story got around
From the crew that found his corpse
And promp'ly laid 'im in the ground.

Just one old nester—more or less
Weren't worth the court's expense
When, the man who brought the story
Owned the town, and common sense
Said to drop the little matter
For his statement must be true
'Cause he sat, each Sunday mornin'
In his custom cushioned pew.

Prowlin' 'round for mav'rick cattle
Fifty years or so ago
Splattered tracks had swiftly led me
Thru the gap, and bendin' low
To dodge some hangin' branches
Noticed marks and flattened lead
Linin' up with open window
Where someone—or somethin', bled.

Diggin' slugs from walls and window
It was plain as widder green
That the feller's sudden illness
Weren't a problem with his spleen
But the time for proper justice
Slid away on gilded wings
For the world just cain't be bothered
With them triflin' sorta things.

So the meadow holds the silence
From the saggin', open door
Solemn keeper of the drama
Lost to time and rotten core
Of a system geared to progress
That no man must dare impede
Lest he find himself a martyr
To the grindin' stone of greed.

The Big Country
By J.N. Swanson
(1927-2014)

Child of the Plains

By Buck Ramsey
(1938-1998)

I write from trees and mountain rocks
There aren't too many on your plain
I think of you and think of grass
That covers place and place again

These trees stretch up to soothe the sight
From seeing far too much too far
As if we could not stand beside
The length we look up to a star

You and I, we cast our loops
And trees will tangle up our throw
And what we catch or might not catch
Will take us time and time to know

The trees like pictures on old walls
Hide fades and scars and what's behind
But I'd as soon your blades of grass
Were underneath, we are its kind

The Hundredth Man
By Steven Saylor

Created from one of my dreams, this painting depicts a group of 99 riders on a mission to cross the great divide in what must be an impossible ride. Inspired by the strength of their union they are seeking one more rider to join their mission. They are looking for "The Hundredth Man."—Steven Saylor

Blue Horses Rush In

By Luci Tapahonso

(For Chamisa Bah Edmo)

Before the birth, she moved and pushed inside her mother.
Her heart pounded quickly and we recognized
the sound of horses running:
      the thundering of hooves on the desert floor.

Her mother clenched her fists and gasped.
She moans ageless pain and pushes: This is it!

Chamisa slips out, glistening wet, and takes her first breath.
      The wind outside swirls small leaves
      and branches in the dark.
Her father's eyes are wet with gratitude.
He prays and watches both mother and baby—stunned.

This baby arrived amid a herd of horses,
      horses of different colors.

White horses ride in on the breath of the wind.
White horses from the west
where plants of golden chamisa shimmer in the moonlight.

She arrived amid a herd of horses.

Yellow horses enter from the east
bringing the scent of prairie grasses
from the small hills outside.

She arrived amid a herd of horses.

Blue horses rush in, snorting from the desert in the south.
It is possible to see across the entire valley to Niist'áá from Tó.
Bah, from here your grandmothers went to war long ago.

She arrived amid a herd of horses.

Black horses came from the north.
They are the lush summers of Montana and still white winters of Idaho.

Chamisa, Chamisa Bah. It is all this that you are.
You will grow; laughing, crying,
and we will celebrate each change you live.

You will grow strong like the horses of your past.
You will grow strong like the horses of your birth.

Sheepherder Blues

By Luci Tapahonso
(For Betty Holyan)

"Went to NCC for a year,"
she said,
"was alright.
There was some drinking, fights.
I just kept low.
It was alright."

This friend
haven't seen for a year or two.
It was a good surprise.
Took her downtown
to catch the next bus
to Gallup.

"I went to Oklahoma City,"
she said,

"to vacation, visit friends,
have a good time.
But I got the sheepherder blues
in Oklahoma City."

"I kept worrying about my sheep
if they were okay
really missed them,
the long days in the sun.
So after 4 days
I had to leave Oklahoma City."

So she went back,
first bus to Gallup,
then a 2-hour drive
to her sheep.

The Gift
By Vel Miller

Pack Mule

By Savanna Scout Cox

I'm a strong girl I can
Throw bags of salt over one shoulder I can
Pick up propane bottles
And baby calves I pushed
The door open like Atlas I shove
400 pound steers I load
Myself down with
Heavy emotion and carry it
Sacks of sugar up and down the staircase
Groceries, books, luggage I hate
To make more than one trip so I ask
Myself if I can take just a little more
I'm a simple girl I'm not
More full of love than anyone else but I feel
A little more resilient I feel
A little more stubborn I have
Broad hips and square shoulders and I can
Carry this by myself farther than
Other girls can carry it without stumbling
I'm a tough girl I don't
Cry out from that kind of pain I don't
Whine about bruises on the outside
Blue and yellow-purple and a hoof scar
It's not much of a burden, really, I wonder
What would happen if I set it down
For a minute I hope
You would hoist it from the ground you would
Raise it to your chest you would
Let me catch my breath and then I could
Take it back.

Alass
By Vel Miller

Waitin' on the Drive

By Larry McWhorter (1957-2003)

It's four o'clock when the cook's bell calls,
Raisin' cowboys up from their dreams.
I pull on my boots and watch the red dust
Come puffin' up through the worn seams.

Spring works are on and we're leavin' 'fore dawn
And we won't strip our kacks 'til night.
As I jingle the horses I wonder
How the bunkhouse looks in daylight.

We're met with growls from a grouchy old cook
As his "sacred shrine" we invade,
But the table's stacked high with good steak and spuds
And fresh biscuits he has just made.

We're no better thought of at the corral
Where the snorts guide our way through the dark.
"Ol' J.J. today," I hear David say,
Ol' Dave's ride will be no gay lark.

The strawboss aims true as we call our mounts,
Ropin' horses his privilege for years
'Cause he knows each horse in the stars' murky light
By "skyin'" the tips of their ears.

Finally we're mounted and ready to go
As the cowboss leads out the way.
We ride by the "wagon," long since retired,
Just a relic of yesterday.

How many good meals were served from its box?
How many good hands called it home?
Though it's been idle for ten years or more
The sight of it stirs young men to roam.

Ol' cowboss, he come here just as a kid
Of sixteen short summers or so.
Raised choppin' rows for his sharecroppin' pa
Till he worked up the nerve to say no.

"I almost went home many times," he'd say.
"Things was tough on buttons back then.
But I'd think of that hoe and that ten yard sack,
Them rough horses didn't look so bad then."

I've heard that old story a hundred times
From men showin' frost in their hair.
Them cotton fields sure made lots of good hands
But I'm happy I wasn't there.

These thoughts and more kinda flow through my mind
As I sit on this caprock so high.
I run my fingers through Black Draught's dark mane
And watch the last star wave goodbye.

Shadows stretch out as Ol' Sol makes his call
Climbing slowly up toward his domain,
And does away with the morn's early fog,
Remnant of last night's gentle rain.

Movement catches my eye from the west.
The herd filters out of the brush.
That outside circle's sure comin' 'round fast.
I'll bet due to J.J.'s mad rush.

Cows callin' calves and hoots from the boys
Are the only sounds that I hear.
Bob Wills' old fiddle playin' "Faded Love"
Ain't as sweet to this cowboy's ear.

Little white faces made bright by the sun
Bounce high with their tails in the air.
That little red calf's chargin' Jake and Ol' Eight
Bawlin', "Come on big boy, if you dare."

And I think as I gaze on the South Pease below,
I really get paid to do this.
My wage is low next to that paid in town
But look what those poor townsfolk miss.

Back Home
By Tom Browning

Well, the herd's gettin' near the draw I must guard,
Like many before me have done.
If I don't get there to head 'em off soon
They'll sure have a long ways to run.

But 'fore I drop off I draw a breath of crisp air,
The kind that brought Adam to life,
And I thank God that He made this feller that's me
As I sit, waitin' on the drive.

Larry McWhorter wrote: "'Waitin' on the Drive' is one of those poems born from a nostalgia of the deep respect a cowboy has for his heritage. So many of the little 'tricks of the trade' which have been unnoticed or forgotten have played an important part in the development of the American cowboy. Riding and roping can be accomplished by almost anyone with little regard for anything except the enjoyment of the moment. I'd be willing to bet, however, there is not a 'cowboy' anywhere, who, upon performing the most obscure of tasks, doesn't take a moment to remember the man, horse or situation which taught him those little 'tricks,' or feel those mentors looking over his shoulder."

The Crossing

By Vess Quinlan

Rolling east in a brand new,
Black and green, Ford 1951
With Uncle Dell and Helen.
I am past ready
For real adventure.
To be a third-grade graduate
And never out of Colorado
Is practically embarassing.
Excitement multiplies as we approach
The border of exotic, mysterious,
Kansas.
I can scarcely contain myself
And not resist asking,
Every other mile or so,
How soon we would be there.

I wonder aloud
If Kansas cowboys speak English
And would know any good poems?
Would there be white-face cattle?
Are there tumbleweeds,
Jackrabbits, rattlesnakes, and centipedes?
How about antelope, are there antelope?

Then in black and white
A sign,
KANSAS STATE LINE.
"Be quiet for God's sake," Dell says,
"And look it over. This is Kansas."
Only Aunt Helen understands,
Leans over to stroke my hair
And whisper, "I was disappointed too,
The first time,
When it wasn't any different."

Weaning at the Babbitt
By Mary Ross Buchholz

Futures

By Vess Quinlan

She watches him practice
Making his loop land flat
And open around the salt block.
He will soon be heading steers
For his daddy at jackpot ropings
And will probably lose a fingernail
Or even a finger
Before he learns to dally.

She watches him follow his dad
Imitating the cowboy's walk
Knows he will return
With an odor of burning hair
Bloodstains on his shirt
Rope burns on his hands
And branding dust everywhere.
But he won't miss
A minute of the action.

He's five now
Squirms away from hugs
That last too long
Has come home green
And sick from chewing tobacco
With the haying crew
And knows a lot of words
His mother never taught him.

He'll get kicked and runover
Drug and stomped on.
She'll patch the places
Where hide is torn away
And worry over broken bones.

He'll all too soon
Be chasing wild cows
And wilder women
She will swallow fear
And hold her tongue
But damn it's hard
Because he's so little
And has such a cute smile.

Sage
By Vel Miller

Passing the Mantle

By Vess Quinlan

How small he was
And how he struggled
With the work;
He irrigated, fed, doctored,
And learned, as I had,
The difference between
Right and close,
Then sought my approval
To validate his knowing.

How strange it seems,
And how right,
That a simple passage
Of time has brought
Us here where I finish
This day of favorite work
And look to my son
For his approval.

In 1908
By Linda Hussa

Billy McCluskey
half-breed
half-horse
hired on
with Miller and Lux
at Soldier Meadows
to break horses.

He just stayed right there
at the corrals.
That's all he did was
break horses.
They'd bring him a bunch,
he'd get 'em started
so you could ride 'em.
They'd bring him
a new bunch.
Halter break 'em,
saddle 'em,
get on and off 'em,
so you could do your work.

Range horses.
Wild horses.

'Course they had cowboys
to ride 'em.
I don't think
it would be exaggeratin' a bit
to say he started a thousand horses.

Last time I rode with him
he had that bleedin' ulcer. Heck!
He couldn't eat enough breakfast
to keep a jaybird alive,
then throw up off his horse
and just ride all day.
I don't know how he did it,
he just did.

From "Tokens in an Indian Graveyard"
Spoken by Lige Langston

Lookin' for a Ride
By Tim Cox

Agave
By Karen G. Myers

A Quatrain
By Omar Khayyám (1048-1131)

A Book of Verses underneath the Bough,
A Jug of Wine, a Loaf of Bread—and Thou
Beside me singing in the Wilderness—
Oh, Wilderness were Paradise enow!

Past Carin'

By Henry Lawson (1867-1922)

Now up and down the sidling brown
    The great black crows are flyin',
And down below the spur, I know,
    Another milker's dyin';
The crops have withered from the ground,
    The tank's clay bed is glarin',
But from my heart no tear nor sound,
    For I have got past carin'—
        Past worryin' or carin'—
        Past feelin' aught or carin';
        But from my heart no tear nor sound,
        For I have got past carin'.

Through Death and Trouble, turn about,
    Through hopeless desolation,
Through flood and fever, fire and drought,
    And slavery and starvation;
Through childbirth, sickness, hurt, and blights,
    And nervousness an' scarin',
Through bein' left alone at night,
    I've come to be past carin'.
        Past botherin' or carin',
        Past feelin' and past carin';
        Through city cheats and neighbours' spite,
        I've come to be past carin'.

Our first child took, in days like these,
    A cruel week in dyin',
All day upon her father's knees,
    Or on my poor breast lyin';
The tears we shed—the prayers we said
    Were awful, wild—despairin'!

I've pulled three through and buried two
    Since then—and I'm past carin'.
        I've grown to be past carin',
        Past lookin' up or carin';
        I've pulled three through and buried two
        Since then, and I'm past carin'.

'Twas ten years first, then came the worst,
    All for a barren clearin'.
I thought, I thought my heart would burst
    When first my man went shearin';
He's drovin' in the great Northwest,
    I don't know how he's farin';
And I, the one that loved him best,
    Have grown to be past carin'.
        I've grown to be past carin',
        Past waitin' and past wearin';
        The girl that waited long ago
        Has lived to be past carin'.

My eyes are dry, I cannot cry,
    I've got no heart for breakin',
But where it was, in days gone by,
    A dull and empty achin'.
My last boy ran away from me—
    I know my temper's wearin'—
But now I only wish to be
    Beyond all signs of carin'.
        Past wearyin' or carin',
        Past feelin' and despairin';
        And now I only wish to be
        Beyond all signs of carin'.

Banjo Paterson and Henry Lawson were writing for the Sydney Bulletin in 1892 when Lawson suggested a "duel"
of poetry to increase the number of poems they could sell to the paper. It was apparently entered into in all fun,
though there are reports that Lawson was bitter about it later.—Margo Metegrano

Blue Mesa Range
By Jim Wodark

Morning on the Desert

By Katherine Fall Pettey (1874-1951)

Morning on the desert, and the wind is blowin' free,

And it's ours jest for the breathin', so let's fill up, you an' me.

No more stuffy cities where you have to pay to breathe—

Where the helpless, human creatures, throng, and move, and strive and seethe.

Morning on the desert, an' the air is like a wine;

And it seems like all creation has been made for me an' mine.

No house to stop my vision save a neighbor's miles away,

An' the little 'dobe casa that berlongs to me an' May.

Lonesome? Not a minute: Why I've got these mountains here;

That was put there jest to please me with their blush an' frown an' cheer.

They're waitin' when the summer sun gets too sizzlin' hot—

An' we jest go campin' in 'em with a pan an' coffee pot.

Morning on the desert! I can smell the sagebrush smoke;

An' I hate to see it burnin', but the land must sure be broke.

Ain't it jest a pity that wherever man may live,

He tears up much that's beautiful, that the good God has to give?

"Sagebrush ain't so pretty?" Well, all eyes don't see the same;

Have you ever saw the moonlight turn it to a silv'ry flame?

An' that greasewood thicket yonder—well, it smells jest awful sweet

When the night wind has been shakin' it; for smells it's hard to beat.

Lonesome? Well, I guess not! I've been lonesome in a town.

But I sure do love the desert with its stretches wide and brown;

All day through the sagebrush here, the wind is blowin' free.

An' it's ours jest for the breathin', so let's fill up, you and me.

*"Morning on the Desert" is from Katherine Fall Pettey's 1910 book, "Songs from the Sage Brush."
For many years, this poem was printed on postcards and reproduced with the comment, "Found
written on the door of an old cabin in the desert." With some detective work and some luck, we
found the author was Katherine Fall Pettey. Through her brother, she had ties to the Teapot Dome
scandal, Billy the Kid, and Pat Garrett. She lived the last decades of her life in a mental
institution.—Margo Metegrano, www.cowboypoetry.com/katherinefallpettey.htm*

Longhorn

By S. Omar Barker
(1894-1985)

They asked me "What's a longhorn?"...
      Well, I didn't tell it scarey—
Just told 'em "Whyn't you look it up
      in some good dictionary?"
But when they come and told me
      that the best that they could find
Was "a Texas cow with lengthy horns,"
      I up and spoke my mind.

Of course his horns was lengthy—
      you could guess that from his name,
But that ain't all his ticket
      to the hall of western fame.
The longhorn steer was covered
      by a hide so tough and thick
That just to get a toe-holt,
      it would take a Texas tick
A steady week of borin'
      every day and every night,
And dull his apparatus
      till he couldn't chaw a bite!

It's true he wasn't purty—
      this Texas longhorn steer—
But them there bony shanks of his
      could plumb outrun a deer.
His backbone was a ridge pole
      that was sometimes sorter swayed.
He fought both wolves and panthers
      with a courage undismayed.
His neck was long and leathery,
      his ribs as flat as planks.
He mostly wore his belly
      kinder tucked up in his flanks.
His shoulder ridge was sharp enough
      to split a hailstone through,
And when it come to hidin' out,
      he knowed just what to do
To make the cowboy trouble,
      both to find and bring him in

Which maybe is one reason
      why them brush hands growed so thin.
His color pattern varied,
      sometimes kinder dull and dead,
But the blood that coursed his rawhide veins
      was reddest of the red.
His hoofs, just like the devil's,
      they was split enough to clack.
Acrost the page of history
      they trailed a deathless track.
His nose could smell a norther
      like a bee can smell perfume,
And when his kind stampeded,
      you had better give 'em room!
He wasn't just a bovine,
      but a wild breed all his own,
With a stubborn love of freedom
      bred in every breath and bone.
He trod out countless cattle trails
      to mark a frontier's dawn,
Till plows and rails and fences
      come along to shove him on.

You ask me "What's a longhorn?"
      Well, just one more word's enough—
The longhorn *made* the cowboy—
      and he made him plenty tough!

Tiger
By Vel Miller

Last Rays
By Ann Hanson

We Never Rode the Judiths

By Wally McRae

We never rode the Judiths when we were gray-wolf wild.
Never gathered Powder River, Palo Duro, or John Day.
No, we never rode the Judiths when their sirens preened and smiled.
And we'll never ride the Judiths before they carry us away.

Cowboys cut for sign on back trails to the days that used to be
Sorting, sifting through chilled ashes of the past.
Or focused on some distant star, out near eternity,
Always hoping that the next day will be better than the last.

Out somewhere in the future, where spring grass is growing tall,
We rosin up our hopes for bigger country, better pay.
But as the buckers on our buckles grow smooth-mouthed or trip and fall
We know tomorrow's draw ain't gonna throw no gifts our way.

And we never rode the Judiths when we were gray-wolf bold.
Never rode the Grande Ronde Canyon out north of Enterprise.
No we never rode the Judiths, and we know we're getting old
As old trails grow steeper, longer, right before our eyes.

My horses all are twenty-some…ain't no good ones coming on.
The deejays and the Nashville hands won't let "Amazed" turn gold
We're inclined to savor evening now. We usta favor dawn.
Seems we're not as scared o' dyin' as we are of growing old.

I wish we'd a' rode the Judiths when we were gray-wolf wild.
And gathered Powder River, Palo Duro, and John Day.
But we never rode the Judiths when their siren's songs beguiled
And we'll never ride the Judiths before they carry us away.

Answered Prayers

By Bill Jones

Jake, the rancher, went one day to fix a distant fence
The wind was cold and gusty and the clouds rolled gray and dense,
As he pounded the last staple and gathered tools to go,
The temperature had fallen and the snow began to blow.
When he finally reached his pickup he felt a heaviness of heart,
From the sound that the ignition made he knew it wouldn't start.

So Jake did what most of us would do if we'd been there,
He humbly bowed his balding head and sent aloft a prayer.
As he turned the key for the last time he softly cursed his luck,
They found him three days later, froze, in the cab of that old truck.

Jake had been around in his younger days and done his share of roamin'
But when he seen Heaven he was shocked—Hell, it looked just like Wyomin'
Oh, they was some differences of course, but just some minor things,
One place had simply disappeared—the town they call Rock Springs.
The BLM had been shut down and there weren't no grazin' fees,
And the wind in Rawlins and Cheyenne was now a gentle breeze.
All them Park and Forest Service folks—they didn't fare so well
They'd all been sent to fight some fire, in a wilderness in Hell.

Though Heaven was a real nice place, Jake had no peace of mind,
So he saddled up and lit a shuck, not knowin' what he'd find.
Then one day up in Cody, one October afternoon,
He seen St. Peter at the bar of the Old Proud Cut Saloon.
Of all the Saints Jake knew in Heaven, his favorite was Peter.
(This line ain't really necessary but it makes good rhyme and meter.)

So they shared a frosty mug or two, or maybe it was three,
Nobody there was keepin' score—in Heaven beer is free.
"I've always heard," Jake said to Pete, "that God will answer prayer,
But the one time that I asked for help, well, He jest plain wasn't there.
Does God answer prayers of some and ignore the prayers of others?
That don't seem exactly square, I know all men are brothers.
Or does He reply randomly, without good rhyme or reason?
Maybe it's the time of day, the weather or the season?
I ain't tryin' to act smart, it's jest the way I feel,
And I was wonderin', could you tell, Pete, what the heck's the deal?"

Pete listened very patiently and when ol' Jake was done,
There was a smile of recognition and he said, "Oh, you're the one.
That day your truck it wouldn't start and you sent your prayer adrift,
You caught us at a real bad time—the end of the day shift.
And 10,000 Angels rushed to check the status of your file,
But you know, Jake, we hadn't heard from you in more than jest awhile.
And though all prayers are answered—God ain't got no quota—
He didn't recognize your voice and cranked some guy's truck in North Dakota!"

Free
By Gary Morton

The Old Cow Man

By Badger Clark (1883-1957)

I rode across a valley range
I hadn't seen for years.
The trail was all so spoilt and strange
It nearly fetched the tears.
I had to let ten fences down
(The fussy lanes ran wrong)
And each new line would make me frown
And hum a mournin' song.

Oh, it's squeak! squeak! squeak!
Hear 'em stretchin' of the wire!
The nester brand is on the land:
I reckon I'll retire,

While progress toots her brassy horn
And makes her motor buzz,
I thank the Lord I wasn't born
No later than I was.

'Twas good to live when all the sod,
Without no fence or fuss,
Belonged in partnership to God,
The Gover'ment and us.
With skyline bounds from east to west
And room to go and come,
I loved my fellow man the best
When he was scattered some.

Oh, it's squeak! squeak! squeak!
Close and closer cramps the wire.
There's hardly any place to back away
And call a man a liar.
Their house has locks on every door;
Their land is in a crate.
These ain't the plains of God no more,
They're only real estate.

There's land where yet no ditchers dig
Nor cranks experiment;
It's only lovely, free and big
And isn't worth a cent.
I pray that them who come to spoil
May wait till I am dead
Before they foul that blessed soil
With fence and cabbage head.

Yet it's squeak! squeak! squeak!
Far and farther crawls the wire.
To crowd and pinch another inch
Is all their heart's desire.
The world is overstocked with men
And some will see the day
When each must keep his little pen,
But I'll be far away.

When my old soul hunts range and rest
Beyond the last divide,
Just plant me in some stretch of West
That's sunny, lone and wide.
Let cattle rub my tombstone down
And coyotes mourn their kin,
Let hawses paw and tromp the moun'
But don't you fence it in!

Oh it's squeak! squeak! squeak!
And they pen the land with wire.
They figure fence and copper cents
Where we laughed 'round the fire.
Job cussed his birthday, night and morn,
In his old land of Uz,
But I'm just glad I wasn't born
No later than I was!

One More Wire Gate
By Don Weller

Madonna of the Prairie
By W.H.D. Koerner
(1878-1938)

My Madonna

By Robert W. Service (1874-1958)

I haled me a woman from the street,
    Shameless, but, oh, so fair!
I bade her sit in the model's seat
    And I painted her sitting there.

I hid all trace of her heart unclean;
    I painted a babe at her breast;
I painted her as she might have been
    If the Worst had been the Best.

She laughed at my picture and went away.
    Then came, with a knowing nod,
A connoisseur, and I heard him say;
    "'Tis Mary, the Mother of God."

So I painted a halo round her hair,
    And I sold her and took my fee,
And she hangs in the church of Saint Hillaire,
    Where you and all may see.

Shadow on the Cutbank

By Joel Nelson

History wrote his epitaph
When barbed wire cut the range
While he was but an embryo
Adjusting to the change

But he was not aborted
By the creaking stretch of wire
And the numbers still are legion
Of the horseback man for hire

His shadow cast at sunrise
On some cutbank wall of sand
Is a mate to the conquistador
In Coronado's band

He is steeped in the traditions
Of those horsemen long ago
He is rumored to be mortal
He will not admit it's so

Since the glory that was Camelot
With her dragons breathing fire
The hero of the world has been
The horseback man for hire

And his glory days aren't over
In spite of all we've read
He is no less than he ever was
No matter what's been said

In the deserts of the high-tech world
He's trailing up his cattle
He will never quit his horses
And he'll never sell his saddle

Droppin' In
By S.C. Mummert

Shorty's Saloon

By Johnny Ritch (1868-1942)
Art by C.M. Russell (1864-1926)

By the trails to the Past, on the Plains of No Care,
Stood Shorty's saloon, but now it's not there,
For Shorty moved camp and crossed the Divide
In the years long dim, and naught else besides

Unfettered by care, unmeasured by time—
Where Innocence formed its first friendships with Crime,
Where Bacchus' wild court held ribaldrous sway,
And Shorty, on shift, stood waiting to say,
      "What's yours, Pard?"

Great herds from the South swept by on the trails,
And stages sped Westward, top-heavy with mails
For camps far beyond, where gold was the lust,
And freighters and "bull trains" send whirlwinds of dust

A deep brand on Memory brings back the old place—
Its drinks and its games, and many a face
Peers out from the mists of days that are fled,
When Shorty stood back of his bar, there, and said,
      "What's yours, Pard?"

No fine drinks adorned that primitive bar,
Just "licker" was served, and that seemed by far
The properest stuff in a place, you'll agree,
Where life flowed and ebbed like the tides of a sea,

That scattered and spread far out on the plain,
And men from the wild—hard men that sin's slain
Had marked like a brand—all stopped there, you see,
And Shorty's brief welcome to each one would be,
      "What's yours, Pard?"

And up from the vast, silent stretch of the range—
From line camps and roundups, and all of the strange,
Lone places in cow-land, men came there to play
In that drama whose artists all lived by the way—

Their skyline of life blazed crimson and gold,
For hope gave them wealth and youth made them bold
And strong in life's strife to dare any task
And "licker" was theirs when Shorty would ask,
          "What's yours, Pard?"

They danced and they drank, and they sang that old song,
"I'm just a poor cow-boy, and know I've done wrong,"
While the click of the chips in the games that were played,
And the sob in the music the violin made

Rang out through the smoke that clouded the room,
For Joy held the top-hand and drink drowned all gloom
The future might hold for him who made gay—
And life filled with sunbeams, when Shorty would say,
          "What's yours, Pard?"

Some tragedies mark those trails to the Past—
Some lone, unnamed graves tell briefly the last
Of the story of those who lived ere the change
From that wild, free life of the Borderless Range—
But Memory's kind grasp holds gently the place,
Its drinks and its games—and many a face
Peers out from the mists of days that are fled,
When Shorty stood back of his bar, there, and said,
          "What's yours, Pard?"

This is from "Horse Feathers." In "Charles M. Russell: The Storyteller's Art," Raphael James Cristy writes that Ritch "had come to Russell's attention as the author of a melodramatic cowboy poem that aches with nostalgia called 'Shorty's Saloon.'" Russell responded with a long illustrated letter including these six watercolor paintings.

Escorting Grammy to the Potluck Rocky Mountain Oyster Feed at Bowman's Corner—A Love Poem

By Paul Zarzyski

(For Ethel "Grammy" Bean)

Lean Ray Krone bellers through a fat cumulus
cloud of Rum-Soaked Wagonmaster Conestoga
Stogie smoke he blows across the room,
"They travel in twos, so better eat them even
boys, or kiss good luck goodbye for good."

Tonight the calf nuts, beer-batter-dipped
by the hundreds, come heaped
and steaming on 2-by-3-foot trays
from the kitchen—deep-fat fryers
crackling like irons searing hide.

And each family, ranching Augusta
Flat Crick country, brings its own brand
of sourdough hardrolls, beans, gelatins,
slaws and sauces, custard, and mincemeat
pies to partner-up to the main chuck.

At the bar, a puncher grabs a cow-
poxed handful—7 of the little buggers—
feeding them like pistachios
from palm to pinch fingers to flick-
of-the-wrist toss on target.

Grammy, a spring filly at 86, sips
a whiskey-ditch in one hand, scoops
the crispy nuggets to her platter
with the other, forks a couple
and goes on talking Hereford bulls.

And me, a real greenhorn to this cowboy
caviar—I take to them like a pup
to a hoof paring, a porky
to a lathered saddle, a packrat
to a snoosebox filled with silver rivets.

I skip the trimmings, save every cubic inch
of plate and paunch for these kernels,
tender nubbins I chew and chew 'til the last
pair, left for luck, nuzzle on the tray
like a skylined brace of round bales.

A cattleland Saturday grand time with Grammy
is chowing down on prairie pecans, then driving
the dark-as-the-inside-of-a-cow grangehall
trail home to dream heifer-fat, bull-necked
happy dreams all night long in my Sunday boots.

One Sweet Evening Just This Year

By Paul Zarzyski

(For Wallace McRae)

Sundown rolling up its softest nap
of autumn light over the foothills, grass
bales stacked two tiers above the '69 Ford cab,
our long-toothed shadow slices east,
mudflaps dragging dry gumbo ruts
back home after one beer
at the Buckhorn Bar quenched the best
thirst I've worked up
all millennium, pool balls
clacking above the solemn
cowmen reminiscing their scripture,
waxing poetic lines to The Legend
of Boastful Bill—*one sweet morning
long ago,* the hands-down favorite. I'll bet
this whole load, that old bard,
Charles Badger Clark, knew the eternal
bent of those words
the instant he scratched them across the open
range of the blank page.
                              Glacial melt
runneling over mountain rock,
moist air swirls in the cab
stirring up three decades of Montana
essences atomized
into a single mist, this horse-cow-dog-grit-
gunpowder-drought-leather-sage-sweat-
smoke-loss-whiskey-romance-song
fragrance settling upon the porous
inner wrist of dusk
unfolding for only a moment
its sweet, unique blossom.

                              And me, tonight
I'm the lucky one along for the ride,
head still sweaty beneath my hat,
a harlequin glitter of hayseed
sticking to my bare arm stretched straight
out the window for no reason
but to know my own pores rising
beneath hair pressed flat
and flowing like grass in crick-bend shallows,
timothy in the side mirror, stems hanging on
with one arm and waving
wild with the other—to golden meadows
and rolling prairie flecked with cattle,
antelope, jackrabbit, grouse,
all grazing beneath one big gray
kite of bunched starlings'
acrobatic flashings over stubble.
                              We mosey home,
me and the old truck, in love
with our jag of good Montana grass—
not one speck of simplistic myth
between us and the West that was, sometimes
still is, and thus will be
forever and ever, amen.

*"This poem just seemed, at first blush, the perfect companion
piece to 'Grammy,' as it's set in the same country—bookended by
two watering holes, 15 miles apart."—Paul Zarzyski*

Eyes on the Horns
By Don Weller

Open Range
By Robert Fletcher (1885-1972)

Western land was made for those
Who like land wild and free,
For cattle, deer, and buffalo,
For antelope and me;
For those who like a land the way
That it was made by God
Before men thought they could improve
By plowing up the sod.

I want the rivers running clean,
I want a clear, blue sky,
A place to draw a good, deep breath
And live, before I die.
I want the sage, I want the grass,
I want the curlew's call,
And I don't want just half a loaf—
I've got to have it all.

These cities seem to ear me down
And I can't stand their roar,
They make me have the itching foot
To get back West once more.
I hate the milling herds in town
With all their soot and grime,
I wouldn't trade a western trail
For Broadway any time.

Just give me country big and wide
With benchland, hills and breaks,
With coulees, cactus, buttes and range,
With creeks, and mountain lakes,
Until I cross the Great Divide,
Then, God, forgive each sin
And turn me loose on my cayuse
But please don't fence me in.

This poem is from the 1936 book, "Corral Dust." Cole Porter bought it for
what became "Don't Fence Me In." Robert Fletcher was an engineer and writer.
He conceived and created the text for Montana's first historical markers.

The Cowboy and the Wheel

By James Barton Adams (1843-1918)

I kin take the toughest bronco in the wild an' woolly West;
An' kin back him an' kin ride him, let him do his level best;
I kin handle any critter ever wore a coat o' hair,
An' I've had a lively tussle with a 'tarnal grizzly bear.
I kin rope an' throw a longhorn o' the wildest Texas brand,
An' in Injun disagreements I kin play a leadin' hand;
But at last I met my master, an' I shorely had to squeal
When the boys got me a-straddle of a
                                        Gol-darned wheel.

It was at the Eagle rancho, on the Brazos whar' I fust
Ran across the durn contrivance 'at upset me in the dust—
Natrally up an' throwed me, stood me on my cussed head,
"Trumped my ace in lightnin' order," so old Ike, the foreman, said.
'Twas a tenderfoot 'at brought it; he was wheelin' all the way
From the sunrise end o' freedom out to San Francisco Bay.
An' he tied up at the rancho fur to get outside a meal,
Never thinkin' we would monkey with his
                                        Gol-darned wheel.

Arizony Jim begun it, when he said to Jack McGill,
There was fellows fo'ced the limit braggin' o' their ridin' skill;
An' he ventured the admission the same feller as he meant
Was a purty handy critter, fur as ridin' bronchos went,
But he'd find he was a buckin' 'ginst a dif'ent sort o' deal
Ef he'd throw his leather leggin's 'crost that
                                        Gol-darned wheel.

Such a slur upon my talent made me hotter 'n a mink,
An' I told him I could back it fur amusement or fur chink;
That 'twas nothin' but a plaything for the kids an' that about
Have his idees sort o' shattered if he'd trot the critter out.
Then they helt it while I mounted, an' I give the word to go,
An' the shove they give to start me wa'n't unreasonably slow.
But I never split a cussword, never made a bit o' squeal—
I was buildin' reputation on that
                                        Gol-darned wheel.

Holy Moses and the prophets, how we split the Texas air,
The breezes made whip crackers o' my somewhat lengthy hair,
An' I sort o' comprehended as adown the hill we went,
Them cowpunchers kep' a yellin', "Stay right with her, Uncle Bill!"
"Hit 'er with the spurs, you sucker!" "Turn her muzzle up the hill!"
But I never made a answer; I jest let the cusses squeal—
My attention was all focussed on that
                                        Gol-darned wheel.

Right of the Road
By Frederic Remington
(1861–1909)

The grade was mighty slopin' from the rancho to the creek,
An' we went a gallyflutin', like a crazy lightnin' streak,
Went a whizzin' an' a-dartin' fust to this side, then to that,
The contrivance sort o' wabblin' like the flyin' of a bat.
I kep' pullin' on the handles, but I couldn't check it up,
Yanked an' sawed an' jerked an' hollered, but the darned thing wouldn't stop.
An' a sort o' sneakin' idee through my brain begun to steal,
That the devil helt a mortgage on that
                              Gol-darned wheel.

I've a sort o' dim an' hazy recollection o' the stop—
O' the airth a spinnin' 'round me an' the stars all tangled up;
Then there come a intermission, which extended till I found
I was layin' at the rancho, with the boys all gethered 'round.
An' a medico was sewin' on my skin whar' it was ripped,
An' ol' Arizony whispered, "Wal, ol' boy, I guess yer whipped."
An' I told him I war busted from sombrero cl'ar to heel—
Then he grinned an' said, "You ought to see the
                              Gol-darned wheel."

It was only discovered in 2014 that James Barton Adams was the author
of this formerly "anonymous" poem, often called "The Gol-darned Wheel."

The Retirement of Ashtola

By Larry McWhorter (1957-2003)

When a day's work is done in the limits of town
A man leaves his job at the site,
Then he meets with his friends at their pet water hole
To watch a big game or a fight.

But on the JA's when the saddles were stripped
And the pleasures of town far away,
They gathered 'round the chuck wagon fire
And recalled the events of the day.

Wild horses was rode and wide loops were thrown,
With no one missing of course,
Then the tales of glory and daring died down
And Boy Blackwell was asked 'bout his horse.

Ashtola the mount of this here account
Was a legend who bore the famed brand.
This rider and steed were performers of deeds
That brought smiles from the hardest old hands.

A big ol' gray horse who was honest of eye.
A range wisened, crusty old bird,
And I've heard it said he'd not met the beast
That he couldn't put out of the herd.

A frustrated cow once used all her tricks
But Ashtola would thwart every plan.
Then she got him in close and a little sideways
So under his belly she ran.

"A lot of horses would have lost her," Boy said
"But Ashtola that cow didn't bother."
"Well, what did he do?" a big-eyed kid bit,
"Why, Son, he went down there and got her!"

Such were the tales of this cagey old horse,
That's why he's remembered in glory.
I leave it to you as to whether it's true
But don't judge 'til you've heard all my story.

The years catch us all and it was clear late one fall
That Ashtola's long race neared its end.
So he was given the heave. The JA he must leave
And ol' Boy must part with his friend.

Somehow that night a gate was left open
And Ashtola escaped in the night.
So when the truck from the soap factory came
The gray horse was nowhere in sight.

Boy turned him loose in a pasture he knew
That was remote and out of the way.
As he slipped off the rope and scratched 'tween his ears
To the tired old horse he did say,

"You'll not wash the face of some snot-nosed kid
I'd never permit such a thing.
You spend your days in the ease that you've earned
And I'll see you come early spring."

That winter they had was the toughest in years
Five northers they seen that was blue.
So when the grass turned, with no small concern,
Boy rode to make sure he'd got through.

The canyons were bare, not a soul anywhere,
And he wondered, "Now where can he be?"
Then he noticed 'fore long that somethin' was wrong,
Neither cow nor calf did he see.

He topped out to look on a big flat below
Of the one corner he hadn't been
And the sight that he seen in that valley so green
Turned his worried frown into a grin.

Ashtola had throwed 'em all in a bunch
And was workin' the herd by hisself.
Then he thought of the years he'd spent on his back,
"That ol' horse never needed my help.

Barn Dance
By Ann Hanson

"Three cuts he had goin' and where he put 'em they stayed,
The cows with bull calves on the right.
The cows with heifer calves stood to the left,
But Boys, here's the curious sight.

"The third bunch was standin' way off to theirselves.
And I wondered, now what could they be?
So I eased down the hill for a closer look
And you'll never guess what I see."

The tension was high among the young bucks
As ol' Boy paused for what seemed like days.
"Well, what was they?" some big-eyed kid bit.
Boy grinned at him, then he said, "Strays."

Legends abound on the Goodnight range,
Some canyons are haunted I've heard,
But the ghosts ceased their mischief and gathered to watch
When Ashtola was workin' the herd.

Peaches and the Twister

By Larry McWhorter
(1957-2003)

Now Peaches had a knack for takin'
Things that wasn't Peaches'.
But then his thefts weren't for the loot
The average outlaw reaches.

For Peaches never robbed a bank
Nor rustled any cattle.
He'd buck a JA cowboy down
And make off with his saddle.

Comes a rider from the breaks
Of Llano Estacado.
Law and luck his own he makes.
He stated with bravado:

"I'd like to ride this pitchin' snide
Who makes you boys so squirrelly.
If Peaches wants to buck me off
He'd best get up durned early."

The cowboss was a kindly soul
Who wished no one no harm
And thought he'd best protect the kid
From broken neck or arm.

"Son," he said, "Ol' Peaches
Ain't just anybody's fool.
We keep 'im mostly for the kind
Who treats their horses cruel.

Working Out Kinks
By Tim Cox

"To those who stray beyond the cinch
And chronically get bolder,
I hand 'em Peaches with the dare
To stick *him* in the shoulder."

The kid was undeterred by this
Unwanted act of grace.
He wanted satisfaction
So's he could have his place

Among the riders of the past
He longed to call companions.
His name to echo off the rims
Of Palo Duro's canyons.

And so it went for quite a spell.
The cowboss got his way
While everybody else got sick
Of hearin' everyday:

"If Peaches wants to buck me off
He'd best get up durned early.
If Peaches wants to buck me off
He'd best get up durned early."

Well, bosses can't be everywhere,
It only seems that way,
And so it happened that he had
To go to town one day.

The strawboss by coincidence
Had somewhere else to get.
The boys were on their own that day
And so the scene was set

To stage the showdown 'tween the pro
Who knew the darker arts
And eager youth, who through mere
   youth,
Equated pride and smarts.

The morning sun was gonna be
Too late to catch the show
So in his stead he sent ahead
The predawn's early glow

For benefit of anxious men
Who'd waited for this day.
The fiddler had his fiddle now.
They'd see if he could play.

The saddlin' was easy.
Ol' Peaches knowed the game.
When you're a wolf who preys
   on bear
They all look much the same.

The kid hitched up his chaps and
   grinned
For soon the world would know
That he could ride ol' Peaches.
Then someone muttered low:

"Ol' Peach looks kinda sleepy."
"Why Jack, I think you're right.
He sure don't look like he got too
Much pillow time last night."

"I'll bet he got up early.
Sometimes he likes to muse
Upon the comin' battle and
The tactics he might use."

These thoughtful speculations
Were ignored but not unheard.
Well, *do or die!* upon the back
Of Peaches and he spurred

From shoulder points to D's just like
The rider that he was.
The air was filled with cheers and dust
And Peaches' dunnish fuzz…

And cowboy, though ascent was
   quick,
The kid's descent was quicker.
He landed in a muddled heap
Like he was full of liquor.

Spilt breakfast, hat and makin's
Littered JA ground that morn.
A gaspin', would-be twister cussed
The day ol' Peach was born.

But soon his disencumbered breath
Came staggerin' back in.
Laughin' cowboys wiped the
   morning's
Breakfast from his chin.

He finally stood on shaky legs,
His vision somewhat blurred.
He looked around and tried to speak
But found his speech was slurred.

"Looks like ol' Peaches got up
Kinda early," finally came
From the lips of this young rider
Who'd set his heart on fame.

He learned a lesson on the day
His reputation peaked.
Be careful wreakin' havoc lest
You get *your* havoc wreaked.

Advice

By Deanna Dickinson McCall

Shaking Out Her Loop
By Jim Rey

The corrals were full enough to bust,
And we'd all had our share of dust.
But, we'd got all the pairs in
And the separating was about to begin.
Our new son-in-law was working the gate
Trying hard to discriminate
When an angry mama came charging up
Mad over the holdup.
Hearing the commotion I rode through the dust
And shared some advice he could trust,
"Son, don't crowd her, whatever you do,
When her head is held high she'll take the fence or you.
Better off to just let stand, cool down a bit
She's not afraid of horse or man, let her have her fit.
It's Nature's way to attack or run, fear and anger is part of life.
I know it's not exactly fun, but, remember she is your wife."

Married Into It

By Patricia Frolander

She'll never last—too much city,
Don't know how he stands it.
Imagine! She don't know a heifer from a Hereford.

Oh my, did you hear about her first branding?
Fed them twelve men a four-pound roast
And two burnt apple pies—she'll never make it.

Taught her to milk the cow, did he?
S'pose that's a sight worth seeing;
That old Holstein will kick her plumb to hell.

Those kids of hers, not enough tendin'.
By the way, did you see her garden?
Rows crooked as a dog's hind leg.

I hear she got some chickens.
Bet she turns green dressing them roosters.
She'll need help.

I never! Who ever heard of naming cows and pigs?
Well them pigs rooted up her garden yesterday
And I'll bet she don't call them by pet names now.

She's had it easy
He built that house right off, ahead of the machine shed.
Hasn't had to do without like us.

That oldest of theirs is turning out all right,
Just like his dad, good breeding.
Those girls will be another story; she'll have her hands full.

I heard she was running the baler.
Now if that don't beat all.
Next thing you know, she'll be running the cows.

He ought to keep her home where she belongs.
She's got no business meddling in menfolk things.
If he hadn't got sick, she'd be tendin' the stove.

Profiler
By Cheri Christensen

Her husband had surgery again,
She and her boy are puttin' up the hay.
I ought to take a hot dish over; she's got her hands full.

Good God, she was over here yesterday
Talkin' to my man about semen-testing bulls!
That poor husband of hers—how does he stand it?

She brought a pie to church supper;
S'pose she don't bake too often though.
I'll bet her house is a sight.

Heard she got a computer.
Don't take no machine to run a ranch
Just common sense, you gotta be raised with it.

Their fortieth wedding anniversary—
Kids are throwin' a party. Guess we'll go.
Good chance to see how the place is holding up.

He and his kin kept that ranch going all these years.
I never! She acts like she owns it or something.
Married into it, she did.

Purple Coyote
By John Bardwell

Instinct

By Darin Brookman

What is it makes your old yard dog
Bay all night at the moon,
In chorus with the wild coyote's
Archaic clannish tune?

By daylight he's content enough
To lay around and nap.
Domesticated by his look
A ward of table scrap.

But nightfall wakens something deep
Where mind and soul convene.
Some age-old longing locked away
Embedded in his genes.

The same thing makes a fella
Who is both steadfast and sane,
Jerk down a rope and join the chase
With slack pitched in his rein.

His slight regard for consequence
Attests to what's inside.
A banner unfurled honestly,
Impossible to hide.

Some know it on the ocean's waves.
Some dig it out of mines.
It finds us on the city streets
Or high up in the pines.

It's played out in the stadiums
For all the multitude,
Or realized in the cedar breaks
In perfect solitude.

That we fool others and ourselves
It matters not at all.
We're ruled by what's inside us
When we hear the coyote call.

The Cowboy's Return

By Rorodore Theofelt

Backward, turn backward, oh, Time with your wheels,
Aeroplanes, wagons and automobiles
Dress me once more in sombrero that flaps,
Spurs, and a flannel shirt, slicker and chaps
Put a six-shooter or two in my hand.
Show me a yearling to rope and to brand
Out where the sagebrush is dusty and gray,
Make me a cowboy again for a day.

Give me a broncho that knows how to dance,
Buckskin of color and wicked of glance,
New to the feeling of bridles and bits
Give me a quirt that will sting where it hits,
Strap on the poncho behind in a roll,
Pass me the lariat, dear to my soul,
Over the trail let me gallop away.
Make me a cowboy again for a day.

Thunder of hoofs on the range as you ride
Hissing of iron and the smoking of hide,
Bellow of cattle, and snort of cayuse
Shorthorns from Texas as wild as the deuce;
Midnight stampede, and the milling of herds
Yells of the cowmen too angry for words
Right in the thick of it all I would stay.
Make me a cowboy again for a day.

Under the star-studded canopy vast
Campfire and coffee and comfort at last.
(Bacon that sizzles and crisps in the pan
After the roundup smells good to a man.)
Stories of ranchers and rustlers retold
Over the pipes as the embers grow cold—
These are the tunes that old memories play,
Make me a cowboy again for a day.

Spooked
By Jim Wodark

Roping the Palomino, 1908
By Maynard Dixon
(1875-1946)

111

Tyrone and Tyree

By Jay Snider

I've learned lots of lessons
'Bout cowboyin' up
'Cause I've been a cowboy
Since I was a pup

And my dad taught me
Just like his dad taught him
Rewards without effort
Come seldom and slim

And if workin' for wages
Or bossin' a crew
A job left half finished
Reflects upon you

And good leaders of men
Who while bossin' the crew
Won't ask of their men
What they wouldn't do

'Cause men are just men
And it's by God's design
We all pull on our britches
One leg at a time

But some men are leaders
While others hold back
They stray off the trail
And are hard to untrack

But with proper persuasion
Will likely fall in
'Cause that's just the nature
Of hosses and men

Horsepower
By Bonnie Conrad

Which put me to thinkin'
'Bout Tyrone and Tyree
The best team of Belgiums
You ever did see

Why they'd lay in those collars
And pull stride for stride
Work sunup to sundown
'Til the day that they died

But Tyree would get balky
Not pull like he should
So Tyrone would reach over
And scold him right good

Then the load they were pullin'
Would even right out
That's the lesson in life
That I'm talkin' about

'Cause some hosses are leaders
While some will pull back
They'll stray off the trail
And are hard to untrack

But with proper persuasion
Will likely fall in
See, that's just the nature
Of hosses and men

Which put me to thinkin'
'Bout what Dad had said
And a couple of visions
Then danced in my head

In my mirror, while shavin'
Which one will I see
Could I be Tyrone
Or would I be Tyree

And to leaders of men
Let's all raise a cup
Here's to pullin' your weight
And to cowboyin' up

Writing My Way Through

By Amy Hale Auker

Sometimes I just want to be a girl,
I don't want to be so tough…
I want to turn and ride to the house,
Say, hey boys, I've had enough.

Sometimes I want to wear lip gloss
Instead of this mustache made of dirt,
Wear something pretty and slinky and pink
Instead of these chaps and denim shirt.

Sometimes I want to pull up
Instead of going crashing through the brush,
Say, "Sorry, Honey, I didn't get there in time,
But you know how I hate to rush!"

Some days I count the pairs in the pen
And I don't want to head them all.
I don't want to mill in the dust and smoke,
And listen to those babies bawl.

Sometimes I want to sleep in my own bed
Instead of wrapped in canvas and wool,
But to give up this glorious job
I'd be three kinds of a fool.

For it is often through miles and testing
That a girl can find her strong,
And sometimes, the most beautiful beauty
Comes from days that are hard and long.

And these cowboy days have taught me well
About some other parts of life,
Like kids and love and trails and logic
And don't ever forget your pocketknife.

The truth is that I like these cows.
I like how they move through the world.
I like to be in the wide outside
And don't care if my hair is curled.

So, tomorrow I will saddle right up
And ride no matter the weather.
I'll pull on my boots, don my hat,
And fill my hands with leather.

I'll look deeper than the dirt and sweat,
Show up to ride all day,
Try to treasure the moments money can't buy,
Count those as the bulk of my pay.

Sometimes I just want to be a girl,
I don't want to be so tough…
But as I put these words on the page,
I figure, I'm tough enough.

Cowgirl Country
By Nancy Boren

Pushing 'Em Off the Mesa
By Tim Cox

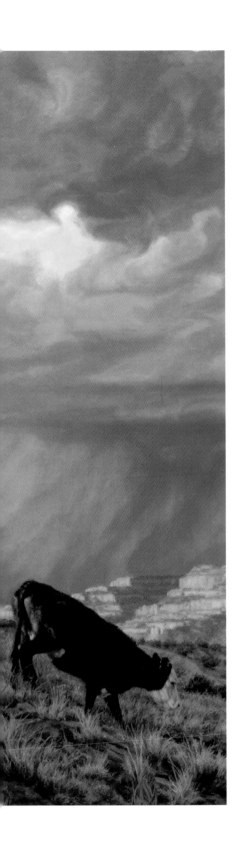

Kinda Like Dancing

By Peggy Godfrey

There's more to building fence
Than hanging up a wire
More to ranching in the West
Than money or desire.

There's more to moving cattle
Than opening up a gate
More to winter feeding
Than hefting all that weight.

There's more to calving heifers
Than luck and calving chains
And more to growing pasture
Than waiting for the rains.

I know the work looks simple
To those who pass us by
But it takes an inner yearning
And a stockman's watchful eye.

It's moving with the rhythms
Of the seasons, nights and days
It's learning land and livestock
To feel and know their ways.

Takes a love for Mother Nature
And the natural way of things
To harvest in the kind of wealth
This life of ranching brings.

Wagon Train

By William Henry Jackson
(1843-1942)

September 7, 1846

By Ruth Whitman
(1922-1999)

Across the white plain of salt
I see an army of wagons
teams dogs children
passing near the horizon
and rejoice to think
another company
is breaking way for us
heading towards the water

and I see a woman:
long skirted in a bonnet
and beside her another woman
multiplied twenty times

who turns who stops
begins again even as I
turn stop begin
and then I understand

how the need for another being
is turned back on oneself
even as rays of heat
turn back and curve upward
against the reflected image

we discover we are traveling
beside no one
but ourselves

Hats Off to the Cowboy

By Red Steagall

The city folks think that it's over.
The cowboy has outlived his time—
An old worn-out relic, a thing of the past,
But the truth is, he's still in his prime.

The cowboy's the image of freedom,
The hard-ridin' boss of the range.
His trade is a fair one, he fights for what's right,
And his ethics aren't subject to change.

He still tips his hat to the ladies,
Let's you water first at the pond.
He believes a day's pay is worth a day's work,
And his handshake and word are his bond.

Bunched Up
By S.C. Mummert

Thirsty Cowboy

By S. Omar Barker (1894–1985)

There's a sayin' out West, and it's true, I'll allow,
That a man who can't drink from the track of a cow
Ain't much of a cowboy; for where punchers ride,
There ain't babblin' brooklets on every side,
For a waddy to drink from when joggin' around.
He waters, like cattle, wherever it's found.
Sometimes there is gyp in the water he drinks;
Sometimes it is muddy, and sometimes it stinks.
Sometimes it's so thick where the cattle have pawed
That before it is swallered it has to be chawed.

But speakin' of water and cowpuncher thirst,
I'll tell you when cowpokes get thirsty the worst.
It's when, at a slow walk that's known as *andante,*
He's passin' in sight of some homesteader's shanty,
And yonder beneath a blue sunbonnet shows
The face of a nester gal hangin' out clothes.
Or maybe he glimpses her framed in the door,
Her yaller hair gleamin' like gold-bearin' ore,
And all of a sudden her face looks so pink,
His terrible thirst makes him stop for a drink.

He may have just drunk from a spring cold and clear
A half a mile back—and the drink he'll get here
May be tanky-warm; but the dipper it's in
Is handed to him by a gal with a grin
That's sure mighty friendly—though modest and shy.
So he drinks and he drinks like he sure 'nough was dry.

Then maybe he lingers a minute or two
And talks about horses, the way cowboys do,
Until, by the time he gets ready to leave,
She's noticed a button that's loose on his sleeve.
So she sews it back on. Well, that's how it goes
When a cowboy sees a nester gal hangin' out clothes!
For nothin' else makes him so thirsty for water
As a glimpse of a homesteader's pretty young daughter.

Straight From the Well
By Tim Cox

The Memories in Grandmother's Trunk

By Red Steagall

They came in a wagon from St. Jo, Missouri.
Grandmother was seven years old.
I remember she said she walked most of the way
Through the rain, and the mud, and the cold.

She saw the Comanche. They came into camp—
Not the savage she'd seen in her dreams.
They were ragged and pitiful, hungry and cold,
Begging for salt pork and beans.

They staked out a claim at the Cross Timbers breaks
Where the big herds went north to the rail.
One day a cowpuncher gave her a calf
Too young to survive on the trail.

Their Jersey cow gave more milk than they needed.
The calf grew up healthy and strong.
She staked him that fall in the grass by the creek
And pampered him all winter long.

In April her daddy rode into Fort Worth
With her calf on the end of his rope.
He traded her prize for a red cedar trunk
That she filled full of memories and hope.

I found Grandmother's trunk hidden under a bed
In a back room where she used to sleep.
I've spent the whole morning reliving her youth
Through the trinkets that she fought to keep.

There's the old family Bible, yellowed and worn.
On the first page was her family tree.
She'd traced it clear back to the New England coast
And the last entry she made was me.

I unfolded a beautiful star pattern quilt.
In the corner she cross-stitched her name.
I wonder how many children it kept safe and warm
From the cold of the West Texas plain.

A tattered old picture that says "Mom, I Love You."
Tho' faded, there's a young soldier's face,
And a medal of honor the government sent
When he died in a faraway place.

A cradleboard covered with porcupine quills,
Traded for salt pork and beans,
Was lying on top of a ribbon that read
"Foard County Rodeo Queen."

Dried flowers pressed in a book full of poems,
A card with this message engraved,
"To my darlin' wife on our twenty-fifth year,"
And some old stamps my grandfather saved.

The New World
By Tom Browning

Of course there are pictures of her daddy's folks.
They sure did look proper and prim.
I reckon if they were to come back to life,
We'd look just as funny to them.

Grandmother's life seemed so simple and slow,
But the world started changin' too soon.
She heard the first radio, saw the first car,
And lived to see men on the moon.

Life on this planet is still marching on
And I hope that my grandchildren see
My side of life through the trinkets I've saved
The way Grandmother's trunk does for me.

"Rancher Duane Johnson and I were standing in front of the Sheraton Hotel in Wichita Falls, Texas, talking about his dad, Virgil, and their heritage—Duane's family has been on the same ranch for five generations. Duane mentioned a trunk that his great-grandmother had brought to Foard County in a covered wagon. The family still has the trunk, and it's one of their most prized possessions.

"Both my grandmothers were very important in my life, and the treasures that they collected are not only family heirlooms but are historical documents of the time in which they lived."
—Red Steagall

Long Dusty Days

By Karen G. Myers

Trailing to Summer Range

By J.N. Swanson (1927-2014)

Cowboy Ridin'

By S. Omar Barker (1894-1985)

I've rode where it's wet, I've rode where it's dry,
I've rode the low country and also the high.
I've rode for big outfits as well as for small,
I've rode horses short, and I've rode horses tall,
But ridin' that's *ridin'*, ol' cowpunchers claim,
On ranch and on range is a heap more 'n a game.

I've rode some by night, and I've rode some by day.
I've rode till my bottom felt plumb wore away;
I've rode for good wages and also for pore.
But no matter which, I know one thing for shore:
They don't call it ridin', where western trails run,
Unless there's some cow-work that needs to be done!

I've rode with a headache, I've rode with the itch,
Got throwed off a few broncs that knowed how to pitch.
I've warmed a few saddles with frost on my pants,
And rode through a blizzard to git to a dance,
But cowboys had just as well ride in a hack
As ride with no ketch rope attached to their kack,
To use, if they need to, on cow, calf, or steer,
For ridin' ain't ridin' without ridin' gear!

I've rode where it's calm, and I've rode where it blows,
I've rode in parades at rodeo shows,
But ridin' ain't *ridin'*, ol' cowpunchers claim,
Without cows to punch—and I figger the same:
From Bighorn, Montana, to old Albukirk,
When cowfolks say "ridin'," they're speakin' of *work*!

The Cowboy's Soliloquy

By Curley Fletcher (1892-1954)

I've ridden afar on the trails of life;
And whether I've been right er wrong
In saddlin' the pleasure, ropin' the strife—
I've "follered" the trail right along.

If I ain't got very much knowledge
Of "literchure," "figgers," an' such,
It's because I "growed" up at "cow" college,
Where book "larnin'" don't count fer much.

My youth now is some dim an' distant,
As I'm "jest sorta" on the down grade,
An' old Father Time gets insistent
Yet—I don't 'pear to feel much afraid.

Why, if I had my life to live over,
An' was put here to ride this same range—
'Course I can't say it's "allus" been clover—
They ain't very much I would change.

I've played out my hand as I found it;
Busted flushes, an' straits—all the same
I ain't goin' to lay down an' hound it,
Jes' 'cause Time had a seat in the Game.

When Gabriel blows his horn for me,
An' I'm tallied along with the dead,
I don't want no cryin' done o'er me
Ner no branded rock put by my head.

Jes' dig me a hole in a hillside,
An' throw in some gravel an' stones;
'Cause it might be best on the last ride
If the varmints ain't gnawin' my bones.

I've collected what I had comin',
In the years I've been here on earth.
If I don't get to hear a Harp strummin'
I guess I've got all I was worth.

I've paid fer my drinks as I got 'em,
An' I've toted my end of the load,
Ner I never dealt off of the bottom,
As I scattered my chips 'long the road.

I've never been much of a hedger,
So I'll jes' play the board as it lays;
An' I'll take my chance on Their ledger,
When They round me up with the strays.

An' if the devil has got me branded,
When I ride fer the Golden Stair,
An' old Saint Pete leaves me stranded;
They'll be wrong, fer I've allus been square.

The Coyote

By Wally McRae

If you get back off the interstates
And away from urban trends,
You'll find a coyote doesn't have
A multitude of friends.

But I kind of like to see one,
Or hear him greet the day,
He's sort of part of our old West
That's fading fast away.

Though he demands his tribute
I'll let him have his due.
Let him take his cut, and welcome.
I guess it's his world, too.

Coyote, Clown of the Prairies
By Will James
(1892-1942)

The Pot Wrassler

By Curley Fletcher (1892-1954)

How are you there cowboy, I hope you are well,
Jest light from your saddle and rest fer a spell.
Here are the makin's, so roll you a smoke,
Yure jest out uh town and I bet you are broke.

Yuh looks like old hunger was a ridin' yuh hard,
So sit down and eat—you are welcome old pard.
I put a lot uh years at a ridin' the range,
But now I am wrasslin' pots fer a change.

Now I ain't no chef like that Del-mon-a-co,
But I sabes the mixin' of old sour dough.
I sorts all the big rocks out uh the beans,
And I don't wipe the fryin' pans off on my jeans.

Muh chuck is all right, and the wagon kept neat;
If yuh don't like the cookin', yuh don't haf tuh eat.
Oh, I'm a pot wrassler, but I ain't no dub,
Fer I'm close to my bed, and I'm close to the grub.

I'm a leetle bit old, and I don't want no truck
With horn hookin' cattle, ner horses thet buck.
I've rode a long time and my laigs is all bowed;
I've got to the age thet I'm easily throwed.

I got the rheumatics and my hands is all burned,
My joints is all stiff and my belly's all churned.
Now I'm a pot wrassler, yure a-hearin' me shout,
So come on and get it, 'fore I throws it out.

You fellers rope steers to down 'em and tie 'em,
Then I comes along to skin 'em and fry 'em.
I got forty a month, and the cookin' to do,
So I'm all through bein' a cow buckeroo.

When you punchers is out in the blizzard an' storm,
I'm close to the fire, where I keeps myself warm.
So do yure old ridin', you wild galoots,
And I'll wrassle pots, you can just bet yure boots.

125

Soft Light
By Cheri Christensen

Morning Glory
By Rod Miller

Stars punch holes in the dark and
the moon curls on the sky like
a hoof paring from a soft-footed horse
while razor-edged peaks stand
against the ribbon of dawn, a dike
holding the morning from its course.

Atop Long Ridge we squat
and sit and roll and spit. Lies hang
in the air, drifting like powder smoke
from round after round of bull shot.
Sparks glint when steel shoes clang
impatient against stone. Scrub oak

materializes deliberately out of the dim
and quakies on the ridges appear.
Stirrup fenders slap saddle seats,
latigos slide cinches taut. A final brim
tug and chap buckle snug and my rear
meets leather. A hesitant sun greets

the crew. Light crawls slow where
today's gather will take us, away
from Long Ridge and our dark climb.
I glory in our forty minutes there;
glad we arrived too early in the day
(or late at night) to get to work on time.

David

By Peggy Godfrey

Bag of rags
I hate sheep
He says
As he scoops up a newborn
In one hand
Holds the goofy ewe down
With a firm knee
And lets the lamb suckle
He looks up
With a shy half-smile
I guess hate's not the right word.

Canyon Strays
By Tom Browning

Hangin'

By S. Omar Barker (1894–1985)

They had a code on the old frontier,
And most old-timers heeded it.
They never did hang a man, I hear,
Unless they thought he needed it.

One or the Other

By S. Omar Barker (1894–1985)

The man who brags that he never got throwed
Ain't one we much admire.
He's either, as cowpokes long have knowed,
A tenderfoot or a liar!

Ranch Horse
By Jan Perkins

Night Shift

By Peggy Godfrey

Into camper quarters
Where I will spend the night
I carry my thermos and snacks
Turn on the heater and lights.

A handful of heifers remain to calve
Coyotes bark and yowl
Bawling calves and echoing cows
Distant, southwest from corrals.

These heifers, no longer spooky
Scarcely turn at my approach
Even the mice don't hurry
As they hunt for uneaten oats.

Who-who is closer than ever
When I step into the night
I glance at the top of the power pole
But dare not shine my light.

Ah, yes, he's there—I see him
Not as well as he sees me
I speak my human greeting
For the owl has greeted me.

Bunnies play in moonlight
Unfearful as I pass nearby
They treat my presence as part of night:
Moon, stars, me, wind, and sky.

Great Horned Owl
By Thomas Quinn

Break
By J.N. Swanson
(1927-2014)

Mustang Manners

By S. Omar Barker (1894-1985)

If you say that a cowboy got throwed off his bronc,
You sure ain't no range diplomat.
It's much more polite if you merely remark
That he got off to look for his hat!

Digging Potatoes

By Linda Hasselstrom

I

We divided it all, but
my grandmother's shoes wouldn't fit
anyone but me.
                    She'd walked years
to the old stove with firewood,
to the chickenhouse for eggs,
to the pasture to check the cows.

II

We buried her in the fall, dry
grasses blowing on the hilltop.
There were no leaves to rustle; no trees
can grow on that dry hill. The view is clear
to the river, the gumbo hills beyond.
                    We even
divided the bright spring flowers—
the hothouse roses, carnations—that
blanketed her coffin. I dropped a rosebud
as if by accident.

III

Wearing her shoes, I'm digging potatoes.
The sweet, rotten earth smell reaches up;
soil clings to my fingers, to the red
potatoes I drop in the bucket. I expect
to see her face at the bottom of each hole,
hear her voice answering the question
I've barely begun to ask.

Uncle

By Linda Hasselstrom
(For Harold Hasselstrom)

He sips coffee
thick hands wrapped around the cup.
"This generation ain't got no corner on violence."
His sunburned hands, cracked and broken, clench into fists.
"You'd be surprised how many fellas
turned up in their own wells
in the Dirty Thirties."

The drought was less severe, he says,
here where ranchers did not tear the sod with plows.
Most families had enough to eat.
His battered hands fixed fences,
drove the teams swathing hay,
paid out worn bills for the land of those who left.

Now they call him a land baron.
"Quitters," he says. "They gave up.
But someone had to stay—
and that took guts. Men like that
had hot tempers and did
their own law-making."

The Little White Lie

By Chris Isaacs

I pulled in one day at the sale barn
And saw the horseshoer's truck in the yard.
So I pulled on over to visit,
And make sure he wasn't working too hard.

When I got close enough to see him,
The sight that I saw gave me chills.
'Twas a scene out of Dante's Inferno,
Made my head start to spin and to reel.

He had this ol' bay horse sidelined,
With one hind leg pulled up and hitched.
Over one eye was still hanging a blindfold.
On his nose hung what was left of a twitch.

A half-empty bottle of Ace lay on the ground,
And a syringe with the needle all bent.
Big drops of red blood on his jugular
Showed the place where that needle had went.

**Under the Cottonwood
With Bubba**

By Don Weller

134

His ol' bottom lip was sure drooping,
And he had to spread-eagle to stand.
His eyes were glazed over and sweat was runnin';
He looked like a drummer in an acid rock band.

But, a much worse sight yet was the shoer,
Kneeling amid tools scattered round.
His shirt was in shreds and one eye was swollen shut
As he picked up some teeth off the ground.

From the end of three fingers the nails were all gone,
And the bill was ripped off of his cap.
A golf ball sized knot just behind his left ear
Showed he'd been in a hell of a scrap.

I said, "Good night boy, what's he done to you?
Sit down before you faint dead away."
He turned his one good eye toward me,
And these words I then heard him say.

"As a shoer, I done my duty.
I hung iron on everything that flew by.
But pard, it wasn't because of farrier science.
It was just sweat, dirt and cowboy try.

"See I got a phone call this morning.
He asked, 'Could I do four head today?'
I said, 'That will just fit my pistol,
Four head at one stop, that's OK.'

"He said, 'Now one will need a scotch hobble,
And one would need a blindfold.
One would take a good shot of Ace.
And one needs a twitch on his nose.'

"Now I ain't no rookie at this line of work,
I've done a bad one or two in my time.
So I told him, 'Don't worry about it.
Me and them horses will get along fine.'

"When I got there, all four horses was tied
Right here by the side of this shed,
And I got by the first three so easy
That the fourth gave me nothing to dread.

"Now I got to admit that he didn't quite lie,
But he wasn't quite truthful either of course.
'Cause the bad habit that each of these horses had
All belonged to the same damned horse!"

Ode to an Old Cow Horse

By Laurie Wagner Buyer

Touchier than a range colt, old hoss,
you ain't never yet been sacked out good.
All strung out on nerves with city folks
around your only peace is knee-deep grass
and high, clean peaks hugging your sides.

For years they've tried to bring you in
tie you down to the snubbing post of
their bright light world. Stubborn as
a jack mule you ain't never budged, ain't
never given in to sweet words and sugar.

Tail to the wind you stand alone and let
the blizzards blow, 'cuz you'd rather paw
through Colorado snow for a bit o' buried
bunchgrass than accept the baled hay and
windbreak boredom of a steel barred corral.

Don't worry, old hoss, I'll never throw a wide
loop at your head. I'd rather watch you pick
your way across a gravel bar for a drink,
and, if I'm patient enough, see you come to me for
a handful of treats, a scratch on your broad back.

Gotcha Covered
By Bonnie Conrad

Dugout Soddie on the Prairie
By Wayne Cooper

Homesteading in Dakota

By Linda Hasselstrom

It was a typical prairie homestead:
a hundred sixty dusty acres
with not one tree.
Mr. Fisher put up a soddy for his wife, five kids,
and dug a well by hand the first month.
The kids and the woman worked the winch
after the well got below ten feet.

He cut logs
in the hills ten miles away for a solid barn,
log-roofed. Once they were settled he went
to the mines in Deadwood, seventy miles away,
for winter cash.

She stayed in the soddy,
milked the cow, dug out a little garden,
struggling with the sod laced together by buffalo grass
roots. Now and then she'd stop for breath, shade
her eyes, look at the horizon line
drawn smooth against the sun.

Mr. Fisher—she called him that—
came home when he could,
once or twice a month all summer. Neighbors
helped her catch the cow, fight fire, sit up
when the youngest child died.

Once
he got a late start, rode in at midnight.
Fumbling at the low door, he heard struggle inside.
The kids were all awake, pale blank faces
hanging in the dark.

When he pushed aside
the curtain to the double bunk
he saw the window open,
a white-legged form running in the moonlight,
his wife's screaming face.
He shot once out the window, missed;
shot her and didn't.
The neighbors said Black Douglas, on the next claim,
walked for a month like he had cactus in his feet.
The kids grew up wild as coyotes.

He never went to trial.
He'd done the best he could;
not his fault the dark spoiled his aim the first time.

Pants Polisher

By S. Omar Barker
(1894-1985)

They asked me "What's a saddle?"
    So I told 'em it's a kack,
A rig of wood and leather
    shaped to fit a horse's back.
You set up in its middle
    with a leg hung down each side,
Some horse meat in between 'em,
    and that is known as "ride."

I could have stopped right there, of course,
    and saved a heap of steam,
But when they speak of saddles,
    my old eyes take on a gleam,
For the saddle is an implement
    that's bred a breed of man
Who rides the range of history
    plumb back to Genghis Khan.
Two legs was all us humans had,
    but men that wanted more,
They figgered out the saddle,
    and its magic gave 'em four.

The Saracen, the Cossack,
    the Arab and the knight,
The Mongol and the chevalier—
    they all was men of might,
Because instead of walkin'
    like a tamer breed would do,
They climbed up in a saddle
    when they had a job in view.

King Richard was a saddle man,
    and Sheridan and Lee,
And Grant and "Black Jack" Pershing—
    just to mention two or three.
Remember ol' Sir Galahad
    of that there poet's tale?
His pants was saddle-polished
    while he sought the Holy Grail!
Of course them heroes never rode
    no Texas applehorn,
But they're the cowboy's kinfolks,
    just as sure as you are born.

They asked me "What's a saddle?"
    It's a riggin' made to fit
A man (sometimes a woman)
    in the region where they sit.
It's made of wood and leather,
    with a cinch that goes around
A chunk of livin' horse meat
    'twixt the rider and the ground.
It's just the apparatus
    that a cowhand climbs upon
To start his day of cow work
    at the chilly hour of dawn.
It's just a piece of ridin' gear
    that, when it's had a chance,
Has give the world some heroes—
    while it polished up their pants!

Vanishing Point
By William Matthews

Evening Star
By Nancy Boren

Code of the West

By Sandy Seaton Sallee

Ella Liddy Watson stood proud at six foot two
Sparkling eyes and willing smile for all she loved to do
But married to a farmer, Kansas neighbor man
She learned the feel of meanness, and soon she packed and ran.

She cooked across the prairies, heart yearning for the West
There's always work for bakers, and Ella topped the best.
She filed divorce in Denver, then she's Wyoming bound
She'd heard of work in Rawlins, and free homesteading ground.

Cookin' at the Rawlins House, 'til Jim Averell came through
He sparked a fire in Ella, he's a gentleman and true
Down from Sweetwater Valley, owned a farm he'd claimed up there
Ella dreamed of owning land, and all that they could share.

One homestead to a family, that's strict Wyoming code
A wife can't file a separate claim, so to Lander off they rode
To marry there in secret, their love known in their heart
They struck out for the valley, to make a brand new start.

Ella staked a homestead out on Horse Creek near her man
There she ran a store and cookhouse, up north of ol' Cheyenne
She gathered homeless children, who'd found the need to roam
She gave them food and loving, a safe and precious home.

One day in cold midwinter, a wagon train came by
With 26 old mother cows, their calves had sucked them dry
Starved and nearly staggering, frostbit, worn and beat
A buck apiece changed hands and Ella's cowherd was complete.

She fed them and she doctored, she kept them all alive
The calves grew sleek and sassy, and the cows began to thrive
The orphaned kids had chores now, feedin', up at dawn
They nicknamed Ella Cattle Kate, and so their lives went on.

They were settlers, Jim and Ella, just playin' with a herd
But settlers should be farmers, and soon there spread the word
To cattle baron Bothwell, who owned adjoining land
This greenhorn female sodbuster had burned her cattle brand.

Now cattlemen were angry, in 1889
At farmers and homesteaders, for their cabins were a sign
That days of open rangeland, and water left for cows
Could not survive these families, with their grass-destroying plows.

Bothwell seethed resentment, it struck him to his core
A farmer woman owning cows sparked off a cattle war
He staked out skull and crossbones on Jim and Ella's land
The couple just ignored his threats, they dug in for a stand.

Bothwell rode from ranch to ranch, midsummer made his stance
He stirred a mob to back him, and Ella had no chance
He knew she had no papers, on those poor cows she'd bought
So he told a liar's story, and spun his gruesome plot.

The ranchers all believed him, that Ella rustled beef
For Bothwell said her calves had died, and branded her a thief
Tempers flared in fury, this damn woman must be taught
Cattlemen still ran the land, and rustlers soon were caught.

Albert Bothwell led the charge to Jim and Ella's store
The pounding hooves and shouting men were one bloodthirsty roar
Ella's voice was soft yet strong, but still they made her pay
Moaning winds still mark the shame of that hot mindless day.

The ranchers yelled for hanging, their maddened horses raced
The pine was huge and twisted, the ropes were slung in haste
The sun glared through the branches on Ella's blooded bay
Jim screamed and pleaded with the men to let her ride away.

A woman in a hangman's noose was not the western way
Though Bothwell led the cowardice, no cowman thought to pray
There in Sweetwater Valley, that rolling land of fate
The legend born that never dies:
      THE LYNCHING OF CATTLE KATE

A Cowboy Season

By Jo Lynne Kirkwood

Part I
(Spring—In The Pastures)

In March, when the calves started comin'
the ground was still covered in snow.
That night twenty gave birth the temperature hovered
somewhere around three below.

By mornin' six calves were near frozen
and ten never lurched to their feet.
They lay stiff in their membranes of ice and placenta,
and the live ones were tremblin' and weak.

Then when the sun broke over the mountain,
after that night when so many were lost,
the snow hollows crusted, the ground turned to ooze
and you started to long for the frost.

But when the mist rose off from the pasture
clouds gathered, and then the rains come.
And a deep chillin' drizzle damped the back of your neck,
and your hands were so cold they turned numb.

Then the calvin' became a true nightmare,
what with heifers just plain built too small,
calves comin' backwards, that had to be pulled,
and you wondered if it was worth it at all.

You were gruntin' and gaspin' and covered in sweat,
cussin' to drown out the pain,
neck deep in muck and cursin' the sky,
though you knew in July you'd need rain.

Then a little feller you'd thought was left doggie
answered the bawl of his ma,
and thrustin' his head 'gainst that cow's achin' udder
he sucked life from that muddy spring thaw.

And awareness come hard, like the thunder,
with that power that deep knowin' has.
There was no other place you would rather be
than right here, in the spring, birthin' calves.

Part II
(Summer—West Desert Range)

In July, the muck turns to powder.
Waterin' holes crackle like shards
of ceramic, the grass shrivels up,
and livin' just downright gets hard.

You're haulin' water sometimes sixty miles,
buyin' feed when the prices are high,
cursin' the heat and chewin' on devils
spinnin' dust 'cross a cobalt blue sky.

But at night your world fills with shadows,
and the splendor of moonlight and wind.
And evenin's coyotes pass you like ghosts,
and when they hear you singin', join in.

And together your voices will chorus,
low and mournful into that night sky,
like a dirge, or an anthem, with memories entwined
of the words to a child's lullaby.

And it's there, with the starlight and music,
and the clean smell of sage on the wind,

Shadows in the Sage
By Jason Rich

you remember, again, just who you are.
And you know there's no way you'd cash in.

Part III
(October—The Pasture Corrals)

In late autumn gnarled branches remember
their youth, and know they must die,

and at night they moan, and creak and cry out,
and bare tremblin' limbs to the sky.

And in those lost hours 'til the dawnin'
hoot owls hunt, and predators roam,
and out riding nighthawk you look over your shoulder,
feelin' fearful, and longin' for home.

But a coyote's been doggin' your late season calves,
and near the tank a bear print was found,
and the fences need mending, better get to that soon,
'fore your cattle stray off of your ground.

The wind stirs dry leaves in the shadows.
Is that a bruin, a hidin' in there?
Or could be a cougar, warily watchin'—
Or nothin' but restless night air.

"Aw, come on," you mutter, and shake at your shoulders.
"Grab hold, man. This ain't no big deal."
It's just that October's got you feelin' spooked,
and out here the demons are real.

**Part IV
(Winter—High Country Line Camp)**

In those long hollow days of late autumn
when the cold is gathering strength
like a lariat coiled 'round the horn of a saddle
suppressing the power of its length,

Then you pull down your hat 'gainst the chillin',
hunch your shoulders to ward off the wind
and wrap up in lonesome, 'cause you'll face this alone,
and lock up your dreams, burrow in,

Workin' the Open Range
By Tom Browning

to wait out the long cold winter.
You'll tell time by the length of the day,
the duration needed for a piñon elbow
to burn to a powdery gray.

And you'll store up the things that you'll ponder,
sift the chaff and tune your heartstrings,
sort out the worthy, discard the waste,
and make room for significant things

To hold on to, mull over, sustain you,
give repose through the long winter day,
a core to come home to, an essence to trust
when you're lonely, and long miles away

From the peg where your hat finds a welcome,
the hearth where your boots long to stand,
that place you will go when the winter and snow
have drawn back from this high country land.

The Sentry
By William Matthews

Her First Calf

By Wendell Berry

Her fate seizes her and brings her
down. She is heavy with it. It
wrings her. The great weight
is heaved out of her. It eases.
She moves into what she has become,
sure in her fate now
as a fish free in the current.
She turns to the calf who has broken
out of the womb's water and its veil.
He breathes. She licks his wet hair.
He gathers his legs under him
and rises. He stands, and his legs
wobble. After the months
of his pursuit of her, now
they meet face to face.
From the beginnings of the world
his arrival and her welcome
have been prepared. They have always
known each other.

Peaches' Pride
By Vel Miller

MacDuff: A Scot in the Country

By Linda Hasselstrom

They call it retirement, but
just marking boundaries is a big job:
four bowls of water a day.
I get up at six, wake
the woman and her cat,
hustle out to my rounds:
woodpile, bonepile, pumphouse,
spruce, bunkhouse. Cats
appear, strange fruit
in the winter trees.
The snow seems deeper here
than in the city: I'm undercoated white.

Hustle, bustle, pee, to the barn,
the junkshed, plowing snow
with my mustache, barking
so she knows I'm on the job.
I keep checking the woman, watch
her drink her coffee, the damned cat
on her lap. When she drives off
in the pickup, I find that one
can climb too. I watch
the rooster strut inside his pen,
exchange snorts with the gray horse,
sit on the porch in the sun,
cleaning my feet, bay
at the neighbor's truck. But
it's not all rest. On Monday,
the neighbors helped her butcher.
I must bury the bones
of a whole steer.

I liked the city, but I've been around,
seen it all: poets, pretty ladies,
hustlers, bright lights. Spent three days
in a bar one time, bumming peanuts.
I enjoyed it all like a big T-bone.
But I'm no pup; it's time
to be here, with no cars,
no sidewalks. In the country, a dog
can mark his bounds
with no one to complain.

Wee Bonnie
By Jim Rey

"Land and water
are not really separate
things, but they are separate
words, and we perceive
through words."

David R. Wallace
"The Untamed Garden and
Other Personal Essays"

Crossing the Madison
By Jason Rich

A Cowboy's Prayer
By Badger Clark (1883-1957)

Oh Lord, I've never lived where churches grow
I love creation better as it stood
That day you finished it so long ago
And looked upon your work an' called it good.

I know that others find you in the light
That's sifted down through tinted window panes.
And yet I seem to feel you near tonight
In this dim and quiet starlight on the plains

I thank you Lord that I am placed so well
That you have made my freedom so complete
That I'm no slave of whistle clock or bell
Nor weak-eyed prisoner of wall and street.

Just let me live my life as I've begun.
And give me work that's open to the sky.
Make me a pardner of the wind and sun
And I won't ask a life that's soft or high.

Let me be easy on the man that's down;
Let me be square and generous with all.
I'm careless sometimes, Lord, when I'm in town
But never let 'em say I'm mean or small

Make me as big and open as the plains
As honest as the horse between my knees,
Clean as the wind that blows behind the rains
Free as the hawk that circles down the breeze!

Forgive me, Lord, if sometimes I forget.
You know the reasons that are hid
You understand the things that gall or fret;
You know me better than my mother did.

Just keep an eye on all that's done or said
And right me, sometimes, when I turn aside,
And guide me on that long dim trail ahead
That stretches upward toward the great divide.

Lean On Me
By Jim Rey

The Last Great Rabbit Hunt

By Elizabeth Ebert

Back when we first were married
    We were short of cash, and so
We decided we'd hunt rabbits,
    Just to make some extra dough.
Old Sure-Shot with his twenty-two
    And me, the True Believer,
Content to tag along behind
    And act as his retriever.

Those old jacks sure were plentiful,
    We really were in luck
For every four we took to town
    Would bring about a buck.
But we'd not stoop to sell that way,
    We thought it would be nifty
To wait to take them 'til we had
    Some forty-five or fifty.

Then we'd have a celebration,
    Take in a show, no doubt,
A glass of wine, or maybe two,
    And we'd have supper out.
So we hunted through the winter
    Every chance we got,
For back there in the forties
    A dollar meant a lot.

We piled those rabbits on the roof
    On the north side of a shed,
And the last time that we tallied
    We had a hundred head.
And then the blizzards hit us
    And the wind it never stopped.
We shovelled snow and broke the ice
    And pitched hay 'til we dropped.

And just as sudden came the sun
    And a warm and gentle breeze,
We calved those doggone heifers out
    In mud up to our knees.
And on that wind was wafted
    Such a stench across the lot
That, finally, we remembered
    Those rabbits we'd forgot.

Jack
By Cheri Christensen

I said, "Today you'll have to haul
    Your rabbits out of here."
His most ungallant answer was,
    "Those are *our* rabbits, dear!"
And so we made a compromise
    And I, with much foreboding,
Said I would load the rabbits up
    If he'd do the unloading.

I shinnied up onto the roof
    Of that evil smelling shed
And held my breath and shovelled off
    Those hundred stinking dead.
And then we took off for the hills
    Far from our small abode.
So he could fill his bargain's part
    And empty out the load.

I sat there in the pickup
    Content I'd done my share,
But minute followed minute
    And the rabbits still were there.
I couldn't see him any place
    'Til I followed up a hunch,
There, on the ground, my husband lay
    A-chucking up his lunch.

Was this the macho hero
    That I'd tried so hard to win,
This sorry, sniveling sissy
    With the vomit on his chin?

Great was my disillusionment.
    I'd really had enough!
I'd show what I was made of,
    I'd prove that I was tough!

I jumped into that pickup truck
    And grabbed up one big jack,
And fueled by righteous anger
    I hurled it out the back.
But, at that very moment,
    Above the truck's tailgate
Appeared the sickly visage
    Of my wretched, retching mate.

I swear I tried to stay that throw,
    I really tried my best,
But that rank and rotten rabbit
    Hit him squarely in the chest.
I told him I was sorry
    And I tried hard not to laugh,
For the situation's humor
    Somehow missed my better-half.

Full forty years have passed and still
    These memories make us wince.
Let's close the book. Suffice to say
    We've shot no rabbits since!

Metamorphosis

By J.B. Allen
(1938-2005)

He slipped on his slicker
And stepped off the porch
To a world made of water and wind
The hail beatin' tunes
On his battered old hat
From a sky that was blacker than sin

Intent on his trek
To the ramshackle barn
His eye never spotted that cow
Who gave 'im two whacks
With a crumpled up horn
And laid 'im out flat by the sow

Which lay in repose
Midst the soft coolin' mud
And startled by sudden attack
Proceeded forthwith
Leavin' tracks, mud, and slime
Down the length of his now exposed back

Bedraggled and muddy
Incensed to the core
By treatment imposed by his stock
He floundered and struggled
To stand once again
And gaze 'cross the backs of his flock

In somber reflection
Plumb sphinxlike he rose
Drippin' mud and used grass at his feet
Rememberin' days
At the chuck wagon fly
And the summer rain's strong steady beat

"A sodbuster's life
Is a sorry affair"
He intoned in blubbery spiel
"Fer the prosperous life
Of a feller of means
Has shore enuff lost its apeal"

A solemn procession of one
Made its way
To the steps of the rickety stoop
Commencin' to shuck clothes and boots
Hat and drawers
Barin' all to the rain with a whoop

From beneath a crude bunk
Came a warbag untouched
Since he'd put both his hands to the plow
A butterfly's wings
Runnin' poor second best
To the bright metamorphosis now

Ol' sol threw his first beam of light
Thru the trees
And entered a half-open door
The silence of emptiness
Greeting the sun
As futility seeped from each pore

Racin' light made its way
T'wards the west in huge bounds
Touchin' land standin' open and free
Where a cowpony shied
As a shadow appeared
And fell midst the rocks and the scree

Just the mornin' before
His rider was down
With a beast that was tryin' to rise
But the scene and the mood
Birthed a grim little smile
And a gleam in the cowpuncher's eye

The shackles of civilized livin'
Were left
With the chains that imprisoned his soul
Better circumstance
Ain't all it's cracked up to be
If a feller don't quite fit the mold

Waxed Jacket
By William Matthews

Sipping the Cheyenne
By Don Weller

Watchin' Him Drink

By S. Omar Barker
(1894–1985)

When you ride a horse to water,
    Slack the reins and let him drink,
You can learn a heap about him
    That you maybe might not think.
If he kinder blows the water,
    And he drinks in little sips.
He's a dainty, lightsome stepper,
    And he seldom ever slips.
It's ten to one he's kind at heart
    And nickers for his feed;
Don't need no spurs to make him go
    And never hard to lead.

You take a horse that gulps it
    Like his belly couldn't wait,
He's likely stumble-footed,
    But he'll pack a heap of freight.
The one that socks his muzzle
    In 'most halfway to his eyes,
He's hard-jawed to the bridle,
    And he'll never take a prize
For speed nor spizz nor spirit,
    But when all the rest are tirin',
You'll find his guts is rawhide,
    And his legs is made of iron.

The way some ponies skitter
    When you ride 'em to a pool,
You'd think they never drank before,
    The way they act the fool.
But such a horse is handy
    When there's tricky swales to ride.
He just won't never bog you,
    And he won't git alkalied.
You ride a horse to water,
    And the different ways they drink,
May help you git a line
    Upon the ways they act and think.

You set up in the saddle,
    And you sorter figger out
How one's a good one 'cause he's quick
    Another 'cause he's stout.
The willin' ones, the lazy,
    The smart ones, and the dumb—
You ponder on their drinkin',
    And no doubt it helps you some
To understand their habits
    In the way a cowboy should.
But ain't it kinder funny
    That you mostly find 'em good?
Well, no, it ain't so funny,
    And you know it, too, becuz
If he wasn't good for *som'thin'*,
    You'd be ridin' one that wuz!

POETS & PAINTERS

James Barton **ADAMS** (1843-1918) worked for famous Indian scout and poet Captain Jack Crawford from 1890 to 1892 in central New Mexico. Adams later became a newspaper columnist. His poems include "A Cowboy Toast," "The Cowboy's Dance Song," and "A Song of the Range."

J.B. **ALLEN** (1938-2005) of Whiteface, Texas, was a working cowboy for more than three decades. A frequent performer at major cowboy poetry gatherings, he wrote "Water Gap Wisdom" (1990) and "The Medicine Keepers," which received the Western Heritage Wrangler Award in 1998, and recorded "J.B. Allen: Classics, Kindred Spirits, and Treasures."

Katie **ANDRASKI**, author of the poetry collection "When the Plow Cuts," teaches English at Northern Illinois University in DeKalb.

Carlos **ASHLEY** (1904-1993), lawyer, fourth-generation Hill Country rancher, state senator, and Texas Poet Laureate, 1949 to 1951, received the American Cowboy Culture Award from the National Cowboy Symposium and Celebration in 1992. He wrote five poetry books from 1941 to 1992, including "That Spotted Sow and Other Texas Hill Country Ballads" (1941) and "Origin and Decline of the Texas Hill Country Razorback" (1992).

Amy Hale **AUKER** writes and rides on the Spider Ranch in northern Arizona. Her collection of essays, "Rightful Place" (Texas Tech University Press), received the 2012 WILLA award for Creative Nonfiction from Women Writing the West. She has written two novels, "Winter of Beauty" and "The Story is the Thing."

John **BARDWELL** has been painting the high deserts of Nevada for nearly fifty years. He lives in Reno. *johnbardwell.com*

S. Omar **BARKER** (1894-1985) was born in a log cabin on a small ranch in Beulah, New Mexico, the youngest of eleven children. An educator, forest ranger, trombone player, state legislator, and a veteran of WWI, he wrote close to 1,500 short stories and novelettes, 1,200 factual articles, and five volumes of poetry. He won the Western Writers of America Spur Award twice and was the 1967 recipient of the Levi Strauss Saddleman Award. In 1978, he was inducted into the Hall of Fame of Great Westerners at the National Cowboy Hall of Fame.

Virginia **BENNETT** has worked on western ranches since 1971 with husband, Pete. She started colts for twenty years and has drawn cowboy wages on big outfits. She has performed cowboy poetry since 1988 and is often featured at Elko's National Cowboy Poetry Gathering. She has shared her work at the Smithsonian Institution, been featured on PBS

and NPR specials, authored three books of poetry, and edited two anthologies. She and Pete live in Goldendale, Washington.

Wendell **BERRY** is an American novelist, poet, environmental activist, and farmer. A prolific author, he has written many novels, short stories, poems and essays. He is a recipient of the National Humanities Medal and was the Jefferson Lecturer for 2012. He is a 2013 Fellow of the American Academy of Arts and Sciences.

Buckeye **BLAKE** enjoyed his childhood on the rodeo circuit with his father and grandfather, who bred quarter horses, so it's no surprise he so often depicts bucking equines. He lives on a ranch in Texas. *buckeyeblake.com*

James **BOREN** (1921-1990) enjoyed a successful commercial career before being appointed as the first art director of the Cowboy Hall of Fame. He became an early member of the Cowboy Artists of America, and returned with his family to Texas where he continued to paint full time. He garnered scores of awards for his work, which is included in corporate, private and state museums.

Nancy **BOREN**'s first painting, a watercolor, was done at age twelve while sitting next to her artist father, James Boren, as he painted at the Grand Canyon. Since then she has branched out to original printmaking and oil painting. She has exhibited at the National Arts Club in New York, the Gilcrease Museum, the National Cowgirl Museum and Hall of Fame, and many national juried art shows. Her painting, "Aloft in the Western Sky," is part of the permanent collection of the Booth Western Art Museum in Georgia. *nancyboren.com*

Darin **BROOKMAN** lives near Hollis, Oklahoma, near the Red River, where he and his family run a fourth-generation cattle and farming operation. He began writing poetry in 1992 and has recited at the National Cowboy Poetry Gathering. His 2004 book, "Where Sagebrush Grows," received the Will Rogers Medallion Award.

Tom **BROWNING** has been painting professionally for forty years. In 2009, he was invited to join the Cowboy Artists of America. He lives in Powell Butte, Oregon. *tombrowning.com*

Mary Ross **BUCHHOLZ** grew up on a ranch in Sonora, Texas, which her family homesteaded in 1890. Her drawings have garnered the Award of Excellence from American Plains Artists, the Artists' Choice Award at the Heart of the West, National Cowgirl Hall of Fame, and graced the cover of *Western Horseman* in April 2014. She lives near Eldorado, Texas. *maryrossbuchholz.com*

Laurie Wagner **BUYER** is the author of seven collections of poetry, a novel, "Side Canyons," and three memoirs. She has received the Beryl Markham Prize for Creative Nonfiction and the Western Writers of America Spur Award in Poetry. She and her husband, W.C. Jameson, live in Llano, Texas.

Cheri **CHRISTENSEN** was born in farm and ranch country in Enumclaw, Washington. She has been

featured in *American Art Collector, Western Art Collector,* and *Southwest Art.* She lives in Texas. *cherichristensen.com*

Charles "Badger" **CLARK** Jr. (1883-1957) was the youngest son of a Methodist minister of the Gold Rush era who inherited his father's rich speaking voice but not his piety. He spent six years in Arizona, where he fell deeply and passionately in love with ranching, cowpunching and what he called "the last of the old, open range." He was South Dakota's first Poet Laureate. His books include "Sun and Saddle Leather" and "Sky Lines and Wood Smoke."

Bonnie **CONRAD** has lived on western ranches in Wyoming, Montana, Texas, Utah and Oregon while raising six children with her ranch-manager husband, Roger. Her energy and exuberance for ranch life shows in every brushstroke. Roger writes poetry and they became known as the "Pen & Paint Team." She is a signature member of Oil Painters of America, American Women Artists, and American Plains Artists. *bonnieconrad.com*

Wayne **COOPER** was born in 1942 near Depew, Oklahoma, and is of Yuchi descent. He is an internationally known artist, specializing in western art. His upbringing in Oklahoma and Indian roots are the subject of many of his creations.

Savannah Scout **COX** is a fourth-generation rancher, rodeo cowgirl, and poet living on Calf Creek in the Nebraska Sandhills, a place her family has owned since 1904.

Tim **COX** is a fourth-generation Arizonan. When not painting cowboys and livestock, he's out working with them. He is past president of Cowboy Artists of America. *timcox.com*

Maynard **DIXON** (1875-1946), born on a ranch near Fresno, California, moved to San Francisco in 1893. He worked as an illustrator, but is best remembered for his trips to the Southwest and strong linear WPA-era paintings, including the very famous "Scab." He died in Tucson, Arizona, in 1946.

John **DOFFLEMYER** ranches in the Sierra Nevada foothills of California. He began writing poetry at the age of thirteen. He edited "Dry Crik Review of Contemporary Cowboy Poetry," an innovative periodical published by Dry Crik Press, from 1991 to 1994, and blogs at "Dry Crik Journal: Perspectives from the Ranch." He was poet in residence at University of Redlands. *drycrikjournal.com*

Carolyn **DUFURRENA** and her husband, Tim, manage the Quinn River Ranch south of Denio, Nevada. She has written a book of essays, "Fifty Miles From Home: Riding the Long Circle on a Nevada Family Ranch," and coauthored another with Linda Hussa and Sophie Sheppard, "Sharing Fencelines," and a poetry collection, "That Blue Hour." She has regularly performed around the West and at the National Cowboy Poetry Gathering. *carolyndufurrena.com*

Elizabeth **EBERT**, a closet poet until 1989, has published three chapbooks and three books of poetry,

Warming Up
By Mary Ross Buchholz

including "Crazy Quilt" (1997) and "Prairie Wife" (2006), and recorded poetry on "Live at Thunder Hawk" and "Where the Buffalo Rhyme." She has been featured at the National Cowboy Poetry Gathering in Nevada. In 2005, South Dakota Governor Michael Rounds proclaimed "Elizabeth Ebert Day." A South Dakota native, she still lives on the home place where she and her late husband, SJ, settled near Thunder Hawk.

Carmen William "Curley" **FLETCHER** (1892-1954) was born in San Francisco and grew up in Bishop, California. His many occupations included cowboy, poet, musician, rodeo promoter, publisher, and prospector. His most well-known work is "The Strawberry Roan." He said: "Hell, I spent my best years as a cowboy of the old school. I still look back to long days and nights in the saddle, at thirty dollars a month, as the happiest of my existence."

Robert "Bob" **FLETCHER** (1885-1972) was a Montana highway engineer, writer and poet. He wrote books and pamphlets as varied as his collection of poetry: "Corral Dust" (1934), "American Adventure: Story of the Lewis and Clark Expedition" (1945), and "Free Grass to Fences: The Montana Cattle Range Story" (1960), which was illustrated by C.M. Russell.

Patricia **FROLANDER**, rancher and past Wyoming Poet Laureate, has written two books of poetry: "Grassland Genealogy" (2009) and "Married Into It" (2011), which received the Western Heritage Wrangler Award from the National Cowboy and Western Heritage Museum. She left the city to settle with her husband on the Black Hills ranch that was homesteaded by his great-grandfather in 1885. She says, "After 42 years, I've earned my spurs."

Robert **FROST** (1874-1963) said that "a poem… begins as a lump in the throat, a sense of wrong, a homesickness, a loneliness." Born in San Francisco in 1874, he moved to Lawrence, Massachusetts, in 1884 following his father's death. In 1894, the *New York Independent* published "My Butterfly: An Elegy," launching his status as a professional poet with a check for $15. He wrote many of his most impactful

poems from his farm in New Hampshire, and received four Pulitzer Prizes for Poetry and the Congressional Gold Medal.

Peggy **GODFREY** has been ranching near the Colorado-New Mexico Sangre de Cristo Mountains for decades. She has performed for a wide variety of audiences since 1991 and written six books, including "Write Tough!" and "Stretch Marks," and a recording, "Peggy Godfrey Live: Write 'Em Cowboy." A PBS documentary, "A Woman Ranching the Rockies," gives a look at this extraordinary woman, who donated a kidney to someone she hadn't seen in years.

Ann **HANSON** grew up in Wyoming, and has a lifelong love of western life. She has won many awards including the William E. Weiss Purchase Award. "Secrets" graced the cover of *Western Horseman* in September 2014. annhanson.com

Linda M. **HASSELSTROM** is a cantankerous South Dakota rancher who says being thrown, kicked, stomped, bitten, and given concussions by horses and cattle provided her with incentive to write and persistence enough to publish. Her fourteen published books of poetry and nonfiction reflect her love of the land; awards include a Wrangler in poetry for "Bitter Creek Junction." Her most recent poems appear in "Dirt Songs" (Backwaters Press), with Nebraska state poet Twyla Hansen. "No Place Like Home: Notes From a Western Life," essays, was published by University of Nevada Press. She conducts writing retreats at her ranch and works online with writers. windbreakhouse.com

Yvonne **HOLLENBECK** is a multi-award-winning performer who has appeared at every major cowboy poetry gathering. She is also a champion quilter with a popular trunk show that includes her collection of family quilts that span 140 years. She and her husband, Glen, raise quarter horses and cattle in South Dakota. Her books include "Rhyming the Range," "From My Window," and "Where the Prairie Flowers Bloom." She has numerous recordings as well.

Linda **HUSSA** lives in Surprise Valley near the small town of Cedarville, California. She and her husband, John, raise cattle, sheep, horses and the hay to feed them. She is the author of six books, including "Blood Sister I Am To These Fields," which won the Wrangler (National Cowboy and Western Heritage Museum), the Spur (Western Writers of America), and the WILLA (Women Writing the West) awards.

Chris **ISAACS** is a cowboy, packer, humorist, and performer who has delighted audiences across the West. His books include "From the War Bag" and "Rhymes, Reasons and Pack Saddle Proverbs." His recordings include recitations of his poems, cowboy friends' poems, and classics.

Joan Shaddox **ISOM** is a graduate of the University of Central Oklahoma. She is a former assistant professor of English at Northeastern State University in Oklahoma, and was artist/writer-in-residence for the Arts Council of Oklahoma. She is an award-winning novelist, essayist and poet whose work has appeared in many anthologies and literary journals.

William Henry **JACKSON** (1843-1942), after a lifetime devoted to photography and approaching the age of ninety, picked up a paintbrush and produced a series of paintings to illustrate books on the American West.

Will **JAMES** (1892-1942) was born Joseph Ernest Nephtali Dufault in Quebec, Canada. He started drawing at the age of four. He learned to be a cowboy in Saskatchewan in 1910 and worked his way south. While serving fifteen months in prison in Nevada for cattle rustling, he had time to draw and write. Selling his short stories helped him buy a small ranch in Washoe Valley, Nevada, where he wrote "Smoky the Cowhorse." Published in 1926, it won the Newbery Medal for Children's Literature in 1927. In all, he wrote and illustrated twenty-three books, five of which became feature films.

Bill **JONES** moved to Wyoming to fulfill his cowboy fantasy after a career as a police detective. He worked as a dude wrangler, wagon-train cook, leased a small ranch, wrote three books of cowboy poetry, was a columnist for the *Wyoming State Journal*, and hosted a cowboy radio show. "Blood Trails," a collection written with fellow Marine Rod McQueary in 1993, was published by John Dofflemyer's Dry Crik Press. He and his wife raise Black Angus cattle in Tennessee and own the gun and pawnshop in Harlan, Kentucky, that was used as the model for the TV series "Justified."

Omar **KHAYYÁM** (1048-1131) was a Persian mathematician, astronomer, philosopher and poet born in Nishapur in northeastern Iran. He also wrote treatises on mechanics, geography, mineralogy and music. Edward FitzGerald (1809-1883) made Khayyám the most famous poet of the East in the West when he translated the "Rubaiyat of Omar Khayyám." A ruba'i is a two-line stanza with two parts per line, hence the word rubáiyát (Arabic for "four"), meaning "quatrains."

Jo Lynne **KIRKWOOD** is a storyteller, artist, and rural high school teacher who farms with her husband, Michael, near Sigurd, Utah. She often draws inspiration from her pioneering family who settled in the Colorado Strip of Arizona. She comments that her cowboy poetry friends form a "tiny, tight community that is thousands of miles across."

Bruce **KISKADDON** (1878-1950) started out as a young cowhand and rough-string rider in the Picket Wire district of southern Colorado. He worked for legendary Arizona cattleman Tap Duncan for years and also spent time droving in Australia. He published four books of poetry, including "Just As Is" (1928) and "Rhymes of the Ranges and Other Poems" (1947). "Open Range: Collected Poems of Bruce Kiskaddon" by Bill Siems (2007) includes almost all of Kiskaddon's nearly 500 poems.

Henry Herbert **KNIBBS** (1874-1945) was born in Clifton, Ontario, Canada, to American parents. He grew up spending summers on his grandmother's farm in Pennsylvania developing a love of horses and the violin. After graduating college in Ontario at age eighteen, he moved to New York state. Although he was never a working cowboy, he moved to California in 1910 and wrote thirteen western novels and six books of poetry.

W.H.D. **KOERNER** (1878-1938) was born in Lunden, Schleswig-Holstein, Prussia. His parents immigrated to Clinton, Iowa, when he was three years old. Although he had little formal training, he became one of the best-known artists of the Old West, illustrating more than 250 stories and painting over 600 pictures for periodicals. He illustrated a number of books that later were made into films, including those by author Zane Grey ("The Drift Fence" and "Sunset Pass") and Eugene Manlove Rhodes' classic, "Pasó Por Aquí."

Ted **KOOSER** was born in Ames, Iowa. He had a career as an insurance executive before publishing thirteen books of poetry, five nonfiction works on the writing of poetry, and three children's books. He won the Pulitzer Prize for "Delights and Shadows" in 2005 and many other national awards. He served as Poet Laureate of the United States from 2004 to 2006. He teaches poetry at the University of Nebraska-Lincoln.

Henry **LAWSON** (1867-1922), the son of a Norwegian fisherman and an early feminist writer, suffered from deafness and personal difficulties throughout his life. He traveled throughout Australia and New Zealand. He was a frequent contributor to *The Bulletin*, a Sydney newspaper, where he and Banjo Paterson often debated their views of bush life. Lawson accused Paterson of being too romantic. Paterson criticized Lawson's gloomy outlook. Their work inspired generations of writers. In 1966, Lawson's image appeared on Australia's first ten-dollar note.

William **MATTHEWS** was born in 1949 in New York City and grew up in the Bay Area. His professional career began in Los Angeles, designing album covers for Warner Bros. and Capitol Records. The 1994 published monograph, "Cowboys & Images: The Watercolors of William Matthews," chronicles a decade of the artist's work devoted to cowboys and the American West. In fall 2007, Chronicle Books of San Francisco released a second monograph entitled, "William Matthews: Working the West." *williammatthews.com*

Deanna Dickinson **McCALL**, a fifth-generation rancher who came from Texas roots in the 1840s, spent twenty-five years raising her family in the Nevada desert without phone or electricity. She has recited at the National Cowboy Poetry Gathering in Elko and the Texas Cowboy Poetry Gathering in Alpine. She has written three books, the award-winning "Mustang Spring" (2013), "Rough Patches" (2015), and an early collection, "Hot Iron." In 2012, she also had an award-winning recording, "Ridin'."

Wallace **McRAE** is the third generation of his family to run the Rocker 6 Ranch, a 30,000-acre cow-calf ranch in Forsyth, Montana. He is a passionate advocate for responsible use of the land and writes poetry in support of his beliefs. He is also very funny. His books include: "Stick Horses and Other Stories of Ranch Life," "Cowboy Curmudgeon," and "Things of Intrinsic Worth." He has received the National Heritage Award from the National Endow-

ment for the Arts, the Montana Governor's Award for the Arts, and has served on the National Council of the Arts.

Larry **McWHORTER** (1957-2003) was raised on ranches in the Texas Panhandle. He graduated from Clarendon College. He lived his dream of working for big ranching outfits and loved the pure cowboy life. In 1989, he began writing poetry. He was named Cowboy Poet of the Year by the Academy of Western Artists in 1998. In 1999, his album, "The Open Gate," was named Academy of Western Artists Poetry Album of the Year. His book, "Contemporary Cowboy Poetry," received a Westerners International Award and the Arizona Book Publishers Glyph Award.

Rod **MILLER** grew up in Goshen, Utah, where his family ran a small herd of cattle. He rode bareback broncs in high school, college and PRCA rodeos. More than 100 of his poems have appeared in print in *Western Horseman, American Cowboy,* and *RANGE*. He has published essays, articles, short stories, novels and poetry collections. He has received numerous awards, including multiple Spur awards from the Western Writers of America.

Vel **MILLER** attended the Art League of Los Angeles and later taught there. She has been featured in *Contemporary Western Artists, Southwest Art,* and *Art of the West*. She has completed several commissions, including a sculpture of Ronald Reagan horseback as well as a bronze sculpture of Old Duke, Reagan's first longhorn steer. She and her husband, Warren, live on their Central Coast ranch in California. *velmillerart.com*

Waddie **MITCHELL** grew up on the Horseshoe Ranch south of Elko, Nevada, listening to cowboys' stories and memorizing their poems. He left school at sixteen to become a full-time wrangler and chuck-wagon driver. In 1984, he and Hal Cannon organized the first Elko Cowboy Poetry Gathering. By 1994, attendance had soared to nearly 14,000. Mitchell has won numerous honors for poetry and storytelling, including the Nevada Heritage Award. In 2014, his recording, "Sweat Equity," was released, and in 2015, his book, "100 Poems," was published. He has many previous recordings and a book, "Waddie's Whole Load" (1994).

Gary **MORTON** cowboyed as a teen and eventually became wagon boss on the historic Bell Ranch in New Mexico. As one of the founding directors of the Working Ranch Cowboys Association, he remains a WRCA director and chairman today. "I don't just paint for myself, but to honor the working cowboy."

S.C. "Chris" **MUMMERT** grew up camping on horseback in California. Trained in Chicago, he worked freelance jobs including as a courtroom sketch artist for NBC. "I've been wearing cowboy boots and camping with my horse since I was ten. I consider it a complete privilege to be able to get up each morning and paint western subjects for a living." He earned the Joe Beeler Scholarship from Cowboy Artists of America in 2013 and the Haley Library and Historic Center 2015 Purchase Prize. He lives in San Diego. *scmummert.com*

Karen G. **MYERS** was born in Denver. She has been a costume and graphic designer and a financial analyst for the FBI, focusing on oil painting since her return to Colorado after a decade in Alaska. In her youth she was a rodeo barrel racer and enthusiastic horsewoman. She is a member of Oil Painters of America. *karengmyers.com*

Joel **NELSON** runs the Anchor Ranch near Alpine, Texas. He spent thirteen years at the o6 Ranch and as a horse breaker for the King Ranch in Texas and the Parker Ranch in Hawaii. He served in Vietnam with the 101st Airborne Division. After appearing at the second Cowboy Poetry Gathering in Elko, Nevada, he was instrumental in founding the Texas Cowboy Poetry Gathering. "The Breaker in the Pen" is the only cowboy poetry recording ever nominated for a Grammy. In 2009, he received a National Heritage Fellowship for his poetry.

William Henry **OGILVIE** (1869-1963), poet and journalist, was born in Scotland, second of eight children. His father's family had managed estates in the Scottish border country for 300 years. After graduating from college in Edinburgh, he traveled in Australia for twelve years. Horse breaking, droving, mustering and camping out on the vast plains became the salt of life to him. He wrote hundreds of poems that were published in Australian periodicals covering every facet of bush life. In 1901, he returned home, where he published eighteen books of Scottish verse and prose, including "The Collected Sporting Verse of W.H. Ogilvie."

Andrew Barton "Banjo" **PATERSON** (1864-1941) was an Australian bush poet, journalist and author. He grew up in Binalong, New South Wales. In 1890, as The Banjo, he wrote "The Man From Snowy River," a poem which captured Australia's heart. In 1895, a collection of his works was published under that name. He authored two novels, many short stories, and a book based on his experiences as a war reporter, "Happy Dispatches" (1934).

Jan **PERKINS** graduated from Utah State and worked as a magazine and fashion illustrator before turning to fine art. She has participated in many exhibits throughout the West. *janperkins.com*

Katherine Fall **PETTEY** (1874-1951) published "Songs from the Sage Brush" in 1910. Her poems appeared in *Sunset, Outdoor Life,* and *West Coast*. Little is known about her life. Her brother was Albert Bacon Fall (1861-1944), U.S. senator from New Mexico and secretary of the Interior under President Warren Harding. He is said to have "defended the accused killer of former Sheriff Pat Garrett... who had killed outlaw Billy the Kid in 1881."

Lisa **QUINLAN** grew up on her family's ranch in southern Colorado raising sheep, cattle and alfalfa. She learned poetry and the operation of farm equipment at an early age from her father, Vess Quinlan. She has shared her poems and ranch stories at the Elko National Cowboy Poetry Gathering.

Vess **QUINLAN** was born in Eagle, Colorado, and is part of the fourth generation to raise livestock in rural Colorado. He began writing cowboy poetry during a yearlong bout with polio as a boy in 1951.

He ran away from home at age fifteen and attended at least nine different high schools while doing chores morning and night for ranch families. His work has been published in many books and magazines and at online poetry sites.

Thomas **QUINN** lives and paints on the northern coast of California. He graduated from the Art Center College of Design in Los Angeles. A collection of his wildlife paintings are included in "The Art of Thomas Quinn." *thomasquinnart.com*

Kenneth Melvin "Buck" **RAMSEY** (1938-1998) claimed he got his main education in a two-room schoolhouse in Middlewell, Texas. After graduating from Amarillo High School in 1956, he knocked around from California to Canada until he returned to Texas. He cowboyed until he was paralyzed in a horse wreck in 1962. Confined to a wheelchair at twenty-five, he taught himself how to play guitar and started performing the old cowboy songs. His epic poem about cowboy life, "As I Rode Out on the Morning," became an instant classic. "Grass, With Essays on His Life and Work," a commemorative edition and CD was released in 2005. He received a National Heritage Fellowship from the National Endowment for the Arts and two Western Heritage Wrangler Awards from the National Cowboy Hall of Fame for his recordings.

Frederic Sackrider **REMINGTON** (1861-1909) was raised in upstate New York, the son of a Civil War colonel. He moved to Montana at nineteen and after his inheritance ran out worked as an illustrator for *Harper's Weekly*. He became a favorite of western Army officers fighting the last Indian battles and was invited back West to make their portraits in the field to gain them national publicity.

Jim **REY** was raised in California. His work has appeared in *Southwest Art, Art of the West,* and *Western Horseman*. His paintings have been used by Bantam Books for their Louis L'Amour series. He lives in Durango, Colorado. *jimreystudio.com*

Jason **RICH** grew up in rural southern Idaho but sought formal art training away from home. He and his family run a horse ranch in northern Utah. He is a member of the Cowboy Artists of America. *jasonrichstudios.com*

Johnny **RITCH** (1868-1942), known as the Poet of the Judiths, was a former camp cook, prospector, state legislator, and Montana state historian. His 1940 book, "Horse Feathers," was illustrated by C.M. Russell.

C.M. "Charlie" **RUSSELL** (1864-1926) grew up in Missouri watching explorers and fur traders head west. At sixteen, he moved to Montana, worked briefly on a sheep ranch, cowboyed for a number of outfits, and lived with the Blood Indians. He painted more than two thousand works depicting the life and landscape of the western United States and Canada. He was also a storyteller and author.

Jim **SAGEL** (1947-1998) was born in Fort Morgan, Colorado, the eldest of three brothers in a farming family. He moved to Española, New Mexico, to teach at Valley High School, and taught for twenty-two years at various New Mexico universities. He wrote prolifically in both English and Spanish. In 1981, he won Cuba's Premio Casa de las Américas for his Spanish-language collection of short stories, "Tunomás Honey." After suffering from bouts of depression throughout his adult life, he committed suicide at the Sevilleta Wildlife Refuge in Socorro, New Mexico, on April 6, 1998.

Sandy Seaton **SALLEE** grew up in Yellowstone National Park, where she rode horseback among the elk and drove four-up stagecoaches. After cowboying in New Mexico, she returned to her native Montana where she met and married Scott Sallee. They own and operate Black Mountain Outfitters, a wilderness and ranch outfitting business. She has written two books of poetry, including "Montana Magic" (2015), and recorded "Montana Legacy" in 2007.

Steven **SAYLOR** moved West to paint and ended up working as a cowboy for five years. His highly detailed watercolors can take months to complete. His Dayton, Nevada, studio is in an antique railroad car. *evergreenstudio.com*

Robert W. **SERVICE** (1874-1958) was born in England, grew up in Scotland, and yearned to be a cowboy. He arrived in Canada as gold was found in the Klondike, and hired on as a cowboy on Vancouver Island. But he soon returned to the job he had trained for—banking—and that work led him to the Yukon where he wrote about the prospectors in poems such as "The Shooting of Dan McGrew" and "The Cremation of Sam McGee."

Jay **SNIDER** was born and raised in southwest Oklahoma. His grandfather was a Texas Ranger, and his mother was a rodeo queen. He rodeoed throughout most of his early years and now team ropes and raises ranch horses and cattle. He has a book and companion CD, "Passing it On" (with Ken Cook), and two award-winning recordings: "Of Horses and Men" and "Cowboyin', Horses & Friends." He was AWA's Poet of the Year in 2008.

Red **STEAGALL** grew up in Gainesville, Texas, and rode bulls as a teenager, but at age fifteen was stricken with polio. He took up the guitar and the mandolin as physical therapy. His acclaimed books include "Ride for the Brand" and "Born to This Land," which won a 2003 Will Rogers Medallion. He has received nine Wrangler awards for original music from the National Cowboy and Western Heritage Museum in Oklahoma City. He is a member of the Texas Trail of Fame, the Texas Cowboy Hall of Fame, and the Hall of Great Westerners at the National Cowboy and Western Heritage Museum in Oklahoma City. He was named the official Cowboy Poet of Texas by the Texas Legislature and also served as the Poet Laureate of Texas.

J.N. **SWANSON** (1927-2014) worked cattle in his youth and raised and trained horses most of his life. He spent lots of time on big outfits in California and the Great Basin, often showing up with a horse and trailer, ready to work at roundups, cattle drives, or brandings. He was a member of the Cowboy Artists of America. One of his paintings hung in Ronald Reagan's White House.

Luci **TAPAHONSO** was born in 1953 to Eugene Tapahonso Sr. of the Bitter Water Clan and Lucille Deschenne Tapahonso of the Salt Water Clan, one of eleven children. She received her Master of Arts in Creative Writing and English in 1982 from the University of New Mexico, where she currently teaches. Her five books of poetry include "Blue Horses Rush In," which was awarded the Mountain and Plains Booksellers Association's 1998 Award for Poetry. In 1999, she was named Storyteller of the Year by the Wordcraft Circle of Native Writers. She is the Navajo Nation's first Poet Laureate.

Rorodore **THEOFELT**, aka Anonymous. Margo Metegrano of CowboyPoetry.com says: "I found a 1910 printing in *Leslie's Weekly* (and widely reprinted) giving the author as Rorodore Theofelt, obviously a jumble of Theodore Roosevelt. But who was the author? Stay tuned, I have asked some Roosevelt scholars for their input."

Jeanette **WALLS** was born in Phoenix, Arizona, to free-spirit parents who left the family rootless and occasionally homeless. She moved to New York at age seventeen, finished high school, and put herself through Barnard College, graduating in 1984 with honors. In 2005, she published the award-winning memoir, "The Glass Castle," which details the joys and struggles of her childhood. Her "Half Broke Horses: A True-Life Novel," published in 2009, is based on the life of her grandmother Lily Casey Smith.

Don **WELLER** grew up in rural Washington, roping calves in high school and college rodeos. He worked for years as a designer and illustrator for major magazines, the NFL, and the 1984 Olympic Games. He has won numerous awards and is often featured in major shows and publications. He lives in Oakley, Utah. *donweller.com*

Ruth **WHITMAN** (1922-1999) was born in New York City, married three times, and had three children. She was educated at and later taught at Radcliffe College and Massachusetts Institute of Technology. She wrote eight books of poetry, including "Tamsen Donner: A Woman's Journey," which recreates the journal that Tamsen Donner lost on her nightmarish journey to California in 1846. She also translated poetry from Yiddish, was a Senior Fulbright Writer-in-Residence Fellow to Hebrew University in Jerusalem, and a National Endowment for the Arts Literature Fellow.

Jim **WODARK** was raised in Colorado. He is a member of the Oil Painters of America, an Artist Member of the California Art Club, and a Signature Member of the Laguna Plein Air Painters Association. *jimwodark.com*

Paul **ZARZYSKI** is a former bareback bronc rider on the Amateur, ProRodeo and Senior circuits, and a veteran of 30 consecutive National Cowboy Poetry Gatherings in Elko, Nevada. He is the author of four poetry books, six CDs of poetry and music, and is the recipient of the 2005 Montana Governor's Arts Award for Literature. His most recent book is "51," a collection of thirty poems, twenty song lyrics, and one self-interview, published in 2011. *paulzarzyski.com*

Captivated Moose
By Thomas Quinn

I Feared Most the Willows

By Laurie Wagner Buyer

I feared most the willows
that bend where slough met ridge
where willows grew tall, dark cover
for the black moose who bedded there.

Prehistoric bottom feeder, long legs
huge head, tiny brain, she ruled
the trail by virtue of her size and
the fact that she feared no man.

A cold chill comes when she lays
back her ears and wags that vicious
tongue—the lowered head and raised
up roach that means she'll charge.

I feared most the willows
but I saw as I turned that frightful
bend, the black moose reaching
to lick her newborn reddish calf.